A BOOK OF REMEMBRANCE BEING A RECORD OF THE SERVICES OF OLD BOYS AND MASTERS OF WATFORD GRAMMAR SCHOOL WHO SERVED IN THE GREAT WAR 1914-1918.

FOREWORD.

An attempt has been made to record, in the following pages, the services rendered to King and Country by Old Boys and Masters of the Watford Grammar School during the Great War.

The book is divided into three sections: the first contains the names of those who gave their lives for their country, the second is an alphabetical list of all who served in His Majesty's Forces, and a list of decorations completes the volume.

"THE SOLDIER."

If I should die, think only this of me:
  That there's some corner of a foreign field
That is for ever England. There shall be
  In that rich earth a richer dust concealed;
A dust whom England bore, shaped, made aware,
  Gave, once, her flowers to love, her ways to roam,
A body of England's, breathing English air,
  Washed by the rivers, blest by suns of home.

And think, this heart, all evil shed away,
  A pulse in the eternal mind, no less
    Gives somewhere back the thoughts by England given;
Her sights and sounds; dreams happy as her day;
  And laughter, learnt of friends; and gentleness,
    In hearts at peace, under an English heaven.

RUPERT BROOKE.

In Memoriam

✠

ADAMSON, G. V.
AISH, G.
ANDREWS, P. L.
AYLING, E. S.
BEESON, R.
BINYON, H. H.
BIRD, W. M.
BLY, H. J. B.
BOYLE, C. F.
BRIGHTMAN, S. C.
BULL, A. W.
BULLOCK, R.
CAPERN, H. J.
COX, H. H.
CROLL, G. LE MESURIER
CULVERHOUSE, H. H.
DAWES, M.
DAWES, S. F.
DEAYTON, G. T.
DOLLEY, R. C. F.
DUDLEY, N. M. C.
EAST, B.
ELLINGHAM, V. E.
EVANS, G. W.
FAYERS, S.
FLATT, D. A.
FRANKLIN, F. E.
GLEN, D. C.
GOADBY, J. C.
GOSS, E. O.
GREENWOOD, H. T.
GRIFFIN, N.
GRIMES, P. S.
GROVE, L. S.
HALSEY, E. C.
HANNA, J. H.
HARRIS, E. C.
HART, S. W.
HEATHER, J. C.
HEMMING, S.
HILL, A. R.
HODGSON, R. N.
HOLMES, C. N.
HOUSEHOLD, E. S.
IBBOTSON, A.
IBBOTT, A. D.
IBBOTT, B. C.
INWOOD, W. S.
JAMES, H. A.
JOHNSON, D. J.
JONES, C. A.
KEMPTON, R. O.
KIMPTON, F.
KING, H. J.
LEES, S. C.
LOFTS, B.

In Memoriam (continued)

LOFTS, W.
MOFFET, J. L.
MORSE, H. E.
NASH, F. B.
OSBORN, C. H.
PARKES, F.
PARKES, R. L.
PEMBERTON, L.
PINN, T. S.
POSNER, P. E.
PREWETT, B.
RAE, J. A.
RIDGEWAY, R. S.
ROUTLEDGE, L. H.
RUSSELL, F.
SEAR, S. H.
SLADE, E. F.
SMITH, G. B.
SMITH, R. F.
SNARE, D. T. J.
SQUIRE, L. P.
STOTT, E. B.
STRUGNELL, A. C.
TATTON, E. H.
TIPPEN, L. R.
TOMPKINS, C. A.
TRACY, C. J.
TUCKER, W. E.
VALE, C. S. M.
WARREN, F. F.
WATERHOUSE, A. M.
WATSON, C. S.
WATSON, W. N.
WELLER, G. H.
WHITEHORN, J. W.
WILLIAMS, A. R.
WILSON, A.
WILSON, J. A.
WOOLMAN, J. G.
WYKES, C. E.
YOUNG, A. F.

ROLL OF HONOUR.

ADAMSON, GORDON VICTOR. School period: September, 1907, to July, 1913. Rifleman, Queen Victoria's Rifles. Died in Cambridge Military Hospital, 3rd May, 1915.

ADKINS, ALAN KEITH. School period: September, 1906, to July, 1913. Private, 4th Royal Sussex Regiment. Four years. Egypt, Palestine and France.

AISH, GEORGE. School period: October, 1900, to June, 1902. Lance-Corporal, Civil Service Rifles. Enlisted in April, 1915, and went to France in October; in December was wounded and spent four months in a base hospital; took part in the attacks on Vimy Ridge and on the Somme; killed by a shell while helping to consolidate captured ground, 15th September, 1916.

AISH, WILLIAM. School period: September, 1905, to March, 1910. Sergeant, R.E. Served in France and Belgium from November, 1914, until April, 1919.

ALLEN, CLARENCE NORMAN. School period: May, 1910, to February, 1917. Sergeant, 23rd Royal Fusiliers.

ANDERSON, GEORGE REDVERS. School period: May, 1911, to July, 1917. Flight-Cadet, R.A.F.

ANDREWS, BERNARD. School period: September, 1885, to December, 1889. Sapper, R.E. Egypt.

ANDREWS, PERCIVAL LIONEL. School period: September, 1905, to July, 1909. Lance-Corporal, A.S.C. Died on active service at Gaza, Palestine, of dysentery, 9th November, 1918.

ANDREWS, REGINALD MAURICE. School period: September, 1908, to July, 1915. Private, R.A.S.C. (M.T.). Two years, six months. France.

ANKER, ALLEN MUGGLETON. School period: September, 1909, to March, 1914. 2nd Class Air Mechanic, R.N.A.S.

ANNEAR, RICHARD WILLIAM. School period: May, 1897, to December, 1899. Staff-Sergeant, R.A.M.C. (T.F.). Enlisted September, 1914. Western Front, May, 1915, to December, 1918.

ARCHER, CHARLES JOSEPH. School period: September, 1907, to July, 1911. C.Q.M.S., Bedfordshire Regiment. Enlisted September, 1914, and went to France July, 1915; owing to wounds was transferred in October, 1917, to Labour Corps; subsequently posted to Chinese Labour Corps.

ARMSTRONG, WALTER WORSLEY. School period: September, 1910, to July, 1913. Non-Combatant Corps.

ARNOLD, PHILIP HORACE. School period: September, 1910, to July, 1915. Leading Mechanic, R.N., transferred from R.N.A.S. March, 1916, to February, 1919.

ASBERY, GEORGE CONNAUGHT. School period: January, 1914, to April, 1916. Bandsman, 1st Royal Sussex Young Soldiers' Battalion. One year, six months.

ASHWANDEN, SIDNEY WILLIAM LOUIS. School period: April, 1888, to June, 1893. Lieut.-Colonel, R.F.A. Mobilised 4th August, 1914, with 2nd London Brigade, R.G.A. Proceeded overseas in command of "A" Battery, 281st Brigade R.F.A., September, 1915; subsequently commanded 17th, 235th and 75th Brigades, R.F.A.; twice wounded, Somme, 1916, Langemarck, 1917; awarded D.S.O., 1st January, 1918; three times mentioned in despatches.

AVERY, ALAN CECIL. School period: September, 1904, to April, 1909. Lance-Corporal, Acting-Sergeant Instructor in Musketry, Herts. Imperial Yeomanry. Nearly two years.

AYLING, EDWARD STEPHEN. School period: April, 1901, to May, 1904. Sergeant, London Rifle Brigade. Died 24th June, 1918, from illness contracted whilst serving in France. Over three years.

AYLING, GEORGE FREDERICK. School period: September, 1898, to July, 1900. R.N.A.S.

BAKER, STANLEY FREDERICK GEORGE. School period: September, 1910, to July, 1914. 2nd Class Air Mechanic, R.N.A.S.

BANNISTER, HERBERT JOSEPH. School period: September, 1911, to March, 1915. Private, Artists' Rifles.

BARNES, SIDNEY ISAAC. School period: January, 1898, to July, 1901. Sapper, R.E. 1916 to 1919. France.

BARTON, HARRY. School period: April, 1902, to December, 1908. Lieutenant, R.N.A.S.

BARTON-SMITH, ARTHUR. School period: May, 1899, to July, 1907. Rifleman, 16th King's Royal Rifle Corps. 1914 to 1919.

BARTON-SMITH, FRANK. School period: September, 1897, to December, 1904. Captain, 12th Loyal North Lancs. Awarded M.C., 18th September, 1918, "for distinguished service on the Western Front." Three years, eight months.

BATCHELDOR, FRED. School period: January, 1902, to July, 1908. Chaplain to Forces, 1917 and 1918. France and Belgium.

BATCHELDOR, WILLIAM. School period: September, 1904, to June, 1910. Captain, 9th Leicester Regiment. Commanded 64th Light Trench Mortar Battery, 1917 to 1919; mentioned in despatches, 1917; awarded M.C., June, 1918, for gallantry and good work in the Line. Five years' service, of which three years, six months were spent in France.

BAWTREE, EDWARD. School period: January, 1911, to July, 1914. Lieutenant, Queen's Westminsters. Three years, six months.

BEAUMONT, HAROLD WALTER WALLACE. School period: September, 1900, to July, 1904. Corporal, 4th Reserve Battalion, Lincolnshire Regiment. Musketry and Lewis Gun Instructor, Northern Command. Three years.

BECK, HARRY LEONARD. School period: September, 1904, to December, 1909. Private, 19th London Regiment.

BECKETT, LAWRENCE ABEL. School period: September, 1909, to June, 1910. R.N.V.R. (South Africa). German South-West Africa, subsequently German East Africa with naval guns. Discharged owing to malaria.

BECKLEY, FRANCIS EVELYN. School period: September, 1911, to July, 1916. Rifleman, Queen Victoria's Rifles. Two years. Egypt and Palestine.

BEESON, GEORGE WILLIAM. School period: May, 1908, to April, 1910. 1st Air Mechanic, R.F.C., transferred from Herts. Yeomanry. Discharged as medically unfit in March, 1918, after two years, six months' service.

BEESON, PHILIP. School period: September, 1892, to July, 1894. Sapper, R.E. Two years, nine months. Taken prisoner at Jussy on 25th March, 1918; repatriated Christmas Day, 1918.

BEESON, RALPH. School period: September, 1899, to July, 1905. Second Lieutenant, Indian Army Reserve of Officers. Accidentally drowned in the Ganges Canal at Roorkee, 16th February, 1918.

BEESON, WALTER. School period: September, 1899, to July, 1906. R.E.

BEESON, WILLIAM. School period: January, 1898, to April, 1903. Sapper, R.E. Four years, two months.

BELL, DOUGLAS JOHN. School period: September, 1907, to July, 1911. Lance-Corporal, A.S.C. (Clerk). Three years. On Lord Cavan's staff at G.H.Q., Italy.

BELTON, CHARLES DAVID. School period: September, 1912, to March, 1915. Sergeant-Observer; R.N.A.S. and R.A.F., Wireless Section. Two years. Anti-submarine patrols and mine-spotting duties from N.E. Coast seaplane stations and H.M.S. "Argus."

BENNETT, JOHN HENRY. School period: September, 1900, to July, 1906. Private, Canadian Expeditionary Force.

BENTLEY, JOHN ROBERT. School period: March, 1897, to May, 1900. Captain, R.G.A. Four years.

BEST, JOSEPH COPELAND. School period: April, 1895, to July, 1896. Private, 4th Gloucester Regiment (T.F.). September, 1914, to July, 1916.

BILLINGTON, THOMAS. School period: April, 1907, to December, 1913. Private, R.A.F. November, 1917, to February, 1919. France.

BINYON, HARRY HICKMAN. School period: April, 1884, to October, 1887. Trooper, 9th Light Horse, Australian Contingent. Killed in action at the Dardanelles.

BIRD, WILLIAM MILLER. School period: April, 1903, to December, 1905. Private, Loyal North Lancs. Killed in action, 20th July, 1916.

BISHOP, EDMOND HOOKER. School period: March, 1907, to July, 1909. Rifleman, 2nd Queen Victoria's Rifles. Wounded in France.

BLAKE, ALFRED THOMAS SAMUEL. School period: September, 1901, to December, 1908. Private, 1st Herts. Regiment. September, 1914, to March, 1919. Severely wounded in France.

BLAKE, JOHN LUCIAN. School period: April, 1907, to July, 1915. 1st Class Mechanic, R.N., transferred from R.N.A.S. April, 1916, to February, 1919.

BLAND, STANLEY PICTON. School period: January, 1908, to April, 1912. Corporal, Queen's Westminster Rifles; September, 1914, to February, 1918. France. Discharged owing to effects of gas.

BLY, HAROLD JOHN BARBER. School period: September, 1909, to July, 1918. Cadet, Artists' Rifles O.T.C. Joined up 15th October, 1918. Died of pneumonia following influenza, 13th November, 1918.

BOFF, MARCUS CHARLES. School period: September, 1894, to July, 1901. Rifleman, Civil Service Rifles, 1914 to 1916. Lieutenant, R.A.F., 1917 to 1919.

BOXALL, ARTHUR CLARENCE. School period: November, 1907, to June, 1915. Wireless Operator, Mercantile Marine. One year.

BOXALL, WILLIAM JOSEPH. School period: September, 1910, to December, 1911. R.F.A.

BOYLE, CHARLES FREDERICK. School period: September, 1912, to March, 1915. Senior Marconi Operator, R.N.V.R. Died of double pneumonia following malaria, 14th December, 1918.

BRADEN, ERIC WILLIAM. School period: January, 1909, to December, 1914.

BRADEN, NORMAN ASHLEY. School period: January, 1909, to July, 1914.

BRETT, ROBERT ALAN. School period: September, 1909, to March, 1913. Corporal, R.F.A. Five years. Mesopotamia and Egypt.

BRIGHT, ROBERT WILLIAM. School period: September, 1909, to December, 1912. Private, 1st Herts. Regiment. Three years.

BRIGHTMAN, FREDERICK WILLIAM. School period: September, 1900, to April, 1908. Corporal, South African Infantry. East Africa. Discharged as medically unfit after fever.

BRIGHTMAN, HAROLD. School period: April, 1895, to April, 1896. Trooper, Herts. Yeomanry. Nine months abroad. Discharged as medically unfit.

BRIGHTMAN, SIDNEY CHARLES. School period: October, 1894, to July, 1898. Second Lieutenant, R.E. Gazetted in January, 1915, to Northamptonshire Regiment; recalled in July to supervise building of munition works; went to Egypt, October, 1917; killed in action in Palestine, 22nd March, 1918.

BROOKES, KENNETH. School period: May, 1910, to December, 1913. Bombardier, R.G.A. Two years, eight months. Period overseas, September, 1918, to January, 1919.

BROWN, GEORGE BENWELL. School period: September, 1910, to December, 1911. Lance-Corporal, Civil Service Rifles and R.E. (Railway Troops). April, 1915, to May, 1919. France.

BROWN, HAROLD. School period: September, 1906, to December, 1910. Battery Sergeant-Major, R.F.A. (Herts. Territorials). Five years.

BROWN, MACDONALD. School period: April, 1915, to February, 1917. R.N. Wireless Section.

BROWN, PERCY HENRY. School period: September, 1908, to April, 1910. Private, 19th London Regiment. Four years, six months.

BROWN, SPENCER. School period: January, 1905, to December, 1906. Lieutenant, Herts. Yeomanry, 1911 to 1915; 2nd Cavalry Reserve Regiment (Bombing Officer), 1916; Dorset Yeomanry; 17th Machine Gun Squadron, 1918. Egypt.

BROWNE, ARTHUR WILLIAM. School period: September, 1894, to July, 1897. Captain, 9th West Yorks. Regiment.

BROWNE, HERBERT EDMUND. School period: January, 1908, to December, 1913. Second Lieutenant, R.F.C.

BRUTON, WALTER REGINALD. School period: January, 1892, to July, 1896.

BUCKOKE, GEORGE CHARLES. School period: September, 1909, to July, 1915. Leading Signalman, R.N.V.R.; October, 1915, to February, 1919.

BULL, ARTHUR WILLIAM. School period: September, 1903, to July, 1907. Lance-Corporal, Loyal North Lancs. Killed in France, January, 1917.

BULLOCH, ROBERT. School period: September, 1907, to July, 1910. Lieutenant, Acting-Captain, Royal Fusiliers. Commissioned in 1915 and went out to Suvla Bay, where he contracted typhoid; in hospital at Malta; in July, 1917, went to France and was made Acting-Captain in 26th Battalion, Royal Fusiliers; killed in action near Hollebeke, 20th September, 1917.

BUNCE, CECIL ARTHUR. School period: September, 1908, to December, 1910. Rifleman, 9th County of London (Q.V.R.). May, 1915, to May, 1916.

BURGIN, ROLAND WILLIAM. School period: September, 1915, to July, 1918. Officer's Boy Steward, R.N.

BURLEY, LEONARD EDGAR TRETHOWAN. School period: May, 1908, to December, 1910. Second Lieutenant; A.S.C. (Hants. Territorials), 1st Durham Light Infantry and R.A.F. Served with 29th Division throughout the Gallipoli Campaign; with 13th Division in Kut-el-Amarah Relief Force and with R.A.F. in Palestine as Observer.

BURNHAM, STANLEY JOHN. School period: September, 1911, to July, 1916. Cadet, Inns of Court O.T.C.

BURRELL, CECIL ROBIN. School period: September, 1908, to July, 1912. Sergeant, Herts. Yeomanry. Nearly five years' service. Gallipoli and Mesopotamia. Mentioned in despatches.

BURRELL, JOHN THOMAS NEALE. School period: September, 1897, to April, 1899. Pioneer, R.E. Discharged, after a year's service, as medically unfit.

BURRELL, STANLEY NOLAN. School period: September, 1911, to July, 1915. Trooper, Herts. Yeomanry. Three years, six months. Egypt and France.

BUSBY, BENJAMIN HOMER. School period: March, 1900, to April, 1904. R.F.C.

BUTLER, HARRY. Member of the Staff: September, 1912, to December, 1918. Lieutenant, R.N.V.R. Antwerp 1914; interned in Holland.

BUTLER, NORMAN EDWARD. School period: January to July, 1902. Royal Horse Artillery.

BUTTON, JOSEPH CHARLES. School period: May, 1908, to July, 1910. Private, 2nd London Regiment (Royal Fusiliers).

Malta, France, German East Africa. September, 1914, to March, 1919. Three times wounded.

CALLARD, HENRY JAMES PELLETREAU. School period: January, 1898, to April, 1907. Lance-Corporal, 2/2nd London Regiment (Royal Fusiliers). September, 1914, to April, 1919. Awarded Serbian Silver Medal, 1917.

CAMP, DOUGLAS. School period: September, 1908, to March, 1911. Signaller, Herts. R.F.A. 1914 to 1919. France and Palestine.

CAMPBELL, CHARLES WILLIAM. School period: January, 1906, to July, 1907. Lieutenant, 10th Bedfordshire Regiment. Joined 3rd Seaforth Highlanders, September, 1914; fought with Meerut Division at Neuve Chapelle, Festubert, etc.; wounded August, 1915; commissioned November, 1915; transferred to West African Field Force, July, 1918.

CAMPBELL, JOHN MONTEITH. School period: January, 1906, to December, 1910. Captain, 12th Royal Fusiliers. Enlisted in London Rifle Brigade, August, 1914; commissioned at St. Omer, August, 1915; wounded in the Ypres Salient, 1916.

CAPELL, WILLIAM GEORGE. School period: January, 1894, to June, 1902. Lieutenant, 18th London Regiment (London Irish Rifles). December, 1915, to March, 1919.

CAPELL, WILLIAM HERBERT. School period: April, 1884, to July, 1891. Private, 9th King's Own Royal Lancs. 1916 to 1919. Salonica.

CAPERN, HENRY JAMES. School period: September, 1905, to July, 1912. Second Lieutenant, 10th King's Royal Rifles. Enlisted in 2/4th London Regiment (Royal Fusiliers) in November, 1914; sent to Malta, December, 1914, and to Egypt in 1915; commissioned in March, 1917; killed in France, 23rd March, 1918.

CARTER, CECIL ARTHUR. School period: September, 1909, to February, 1913. Captain, 16th Battalion, Rifle Brigade. Five years. Employed on General Staff from August, 1917.

CARTER, HAROLD WALTER. School period: September, 1905, to May, 1910. Lieutenant, 3rd Essex Regiment and Staff. Five years, six months.

CARTER, HAROLD WILLIAM. School period: June, 1911, to July, 1914. Captain and Adjutant, Surrey Rifles.

CASHMORE, ARTHUR LEONARD. School period: September, 1907, to April, 1910. Corporal, 110th Railway Company, R.E. (Special Railway Reserve). France. Four years, six months.

CASHMORE, ERNEST ALBERT. School period: September, 1909, to July, 1911. Sapper, R.E. Signal Service. 1914 to 1919. France, Salonica, Palestine. Transferred to Tank Corps, July, 1918.

CASS, WILFRED DAWSON. School period: September, 1906, to April, 1911. Lieutenant, 3rd London Regiment (Royal Fusiliers). Five years. Malta, Egypt, Gallipoli, France, Belgium. Awarded M.C.

CASTLE, GEORGE DENNITHORNE. School period: September, 1913, to December, 1914. R.A.F.

CASTLE, JOHN WILLIAM. School period: September, 1907, to July, 1908. R.N.

CASWELL, WILLIAM THOMAS. School period: September, 1912, to June, 1916. Private, 3rd Bedfordshire Regiment.

CHALLANDS, MARCUS CHARLES. School period: February, 1906, to December, 1907. Dorset Regiment.

CHAMBERLAIN, DOUGLAS CHURCHILL. School period: September, 1898, to March, 1906. Rifleman, 16th London Regiment (Queen's Westminster Rifles).

CHAMBERLIN, THOMAS CHARLES. School period: April, 1898, to July, 1908. Captain and Squadron Commander; Middlesex Regiment, R.F.C., and R.A.F. August, 1914, to March, 1919. Awarded Air Force Cross for distinguished services in France.

CHANEY, EDWARD FRANK. Member of the Staff: September to December, 1907. Private, Royal Marine Artillery. Invalided June, 1917.

CHILTON, JOHN. School period: September, 1910, to July, 1911. 1st Air Mechanic, R.F.C. Went through the Retreat from Mons; captured at the Battle of the Marne, September, 1914; prisoner of war for four years, two months.

CHRISTMAS, THOMAS LEA. School period: September, 1911, to March, 1915. Signalman, Royal Naval Division. September, 1915, to March, 1918.

CLACY, HENRY GEORGE. School period: September, 1913, to July, 1915. Second Lieutenant, R.A.F.

CLARIDGE, GUY. School period: September, 1908, to December, 1912. Trooper, Herts. Yeomanry. October, 1915, to June, 1919.

CLARIDGE, HUGH. School period: September, 1904, to September, 1909. Private, R.A.M.C. Four years, nine months. France, February, 1915.

CLEMENT, ALBERT REGINALD. School period: September, 1911, to July, 1915. Private, 1st Artists' Rifles. November, 1917, to February, 1919.

COLLEY, HENRY GEORGE. School period: September, 1910, to June, 1915. Private, 6th Royal Sussex Regiment; 1st Home Counties Cyclist Corps; 6th Royal West Kent Regiment; R.E. Wireless Operator at Divisional Headquarters. November, 1915, to February, 1919. France.

COLLINS, HAROLD JOHN. School period: January, 1907, to December, 1911. Second Lieutenant, 33rd Battalion, Machine Gun Corps and 7th Hampshire Regiment (T.F.). Three years. Awarded M.C. for gallant work in the final assault and consolidation of Englefontaine (Forêt de Mormal) in the last phase of the Cambrai—St. Quentin battle, 26th October, 1918.

COOPER, ARCHIBALD. School period: September, 1896, to December, 1900. Sapper, R.E., Signal Service. September, 1914, to February, 1919. France.

CORBETT, GEORGE. School period: September, 1907, to April, 1910. Private, R.A.S.C. (M.T). 1916 to 1919. Italy.

COSWAY, OWEN WILLIAM. School period: September, 1912, to July, 1916. Trooper, Royal Horse Guards.

COURTNEY, THOMAS. School period: September, 1912, to July, 1917. Rifleman, King's Royal Rifles.

COWANS, HENRY. School period: September, 1906, to July, 1910. Private, 9th Royal Fusiliers, attached 36th Trench Mortar Battery. Three years, three months.

COX, HAROLD HENRY. School period: January to December, 1901. Private, 18th Royal Fusiliers. Wounded 23rd April, died 14th May, 1917.

COX, HUBERT ROBERT. School period: September, 1908, to July, 1910. Corporal, 22nd, 17th and 18th Royal Fusiliers. Five years. Gassed at Ayette.

COX, NORMAN LESLIE. School period: September, 1908, to July, 1913. Private, 32nd Battalion, Machine Gun Corps. Two years. Wounded 15th July, 1918.

CRAWLEY, HENRY ARTHUR. School period: September, 1910, to December, 1913. Private, London Scottish, March, 1917, to May, 1918; Machine Gun Corps, May, 1918, to February, 1919. France.

CRICKMORE, BERNARD HENRY. School period: January, 1909, to July, 1911. Leading Mechanic, R.N.A.S.; November, 1915, to March, 1919. Egypt, Mesopotamia and Mediterranean.

CRICKMORE, LEONARD ALBERT. School period: September, 1910, to July, 1912. Leading Mechanic, R.N.A.S. Three years, six months.

CRISP, JOHN HENRY. Member of the Staff since September, 1906. Lieutenant, Suffolk Regiment. January, 1915, to July, 1916, 16th Middlesex Regiment, France; August, 1916, to November, 1919, Suffolk Regiment, India.

CROLL, CEDRIC WILLIAM LE MESURIER. School period: September, 1896, to December, 1902. Lieutenant, R.E.

CROLL, GRAHAM LE MESURIER. School period: October, 1901, to June, 1907. Private, 23rd County of London Regiment. Killed in action in France, 25th May, 1915.

CROLL, IRVINE LE MESURIER. School period: October, 1894, to December, 1900. Second Lieutenant, Royal West Kent Regiment.

CROMARTY, DONALD EVARARD. School period: September, 1908, to April, 1911. Captain, R.G.A. June, 1915, to July, 1919. Palestine.

CRUICKSHANK, ARCHIBALD. School period: January, 1909, to December, 1912. Sapper, R.E. Four years, six months. China Expeditionary Force.

CULVERHOUSE, HENRY HUBERT. School period: September, 1910, to December, 1912. Private, 1st Herts. Regiment. Killed in action, 14th October, 1916.

CUMMINGS, ALFRED GEORGE HERBERT. School period: September, 1911, to April, 1913. Leading Aircraftsman, R.F.C. October, 1915, to March, 1919.

CURTIS, ARTHUR SAMUEL. School period: September, 1909, to December, 1910.

CUTCHEE, EDWIN JAMES. School period: September, 1905, to July, 1910. Corporal, Army Pay Corps, eight months; R.E. (Special Brigade), three years, six months.

CUTCHEE, HAROLD DELMAGE. School period: September, 1908, to December, 1910. Corporal, Civil Service Rifles. Three years, seven months.

DALTON, PERCY. School period: January, 1902, to December, 1908. Second Lieutenant, 3rd Dorset Regiment.

DANELLS, PHILIP FREDERICK. School period: January, 1908, to July, 1914. Leading Seaman, R.N.V.R. Three years, seven months. Torpedoed by submarine, 12th April, 1917.

DAVIES, IDWAL LLEWELLYN. School period: May, 1904, to July, 1910. Second Lieutenant, 5th Light Horse, A.I.F.; 3/9th Middlesex Regiment. Two years, two months.

DAVIES, JOHN BURTON. School period: April, 1902, to July, 1904. R.N.

DAVIES, TUDOR HUAB. School period: May, 1904, to December, 1906. Private, Artists' Rifles; Lieutenant, 506th (Hants.) Field Company, R.E. September, 1914, to April, 1919. Salonica, 1916 to 1919. Awarded M.C.

DAVIS, ALFRED THOMAS. School period: September, 1905, to July, 1908. Motor Transport, 5th Australian Division Supply.

DAWES, ALBERT CECIL. School period: September, 1902, to July, 1907. Captain, R.G.A. France.

DAWES, MORRIS. School period: September, 1906, to July, 1911. Second Lieutenant, 10th Essex Regiment. Enlisted August, 1914, in 9th Lancers; went to France; was wounded and returned to England; went back to France with a draft and was then attached to Queen's Royal West Surrey Regiment; recommended on the field for a commission and gazetted to 10th Essex Regiment; killed in action, 26th April, 1918.

DAWES, SIDNEY FRANCIS. School period: September, 1903, to July, 1908. Second Lieutenant, R.G.A. Killed in Cambrai offensive, 8th October, 1918.

DEARMUN, SIDNEY ARTHUR. School period: January to December, 1910.

DE'ATH, ERNEST. School period: September, 1907, to July, 1911. Lieutenant, 5th Royal West Kent Regiment, attached Queen's. Four years, six months. France and Palestine. Twice wounded, at Loos, 1915, and Soissons, 1918. Awarded D.C.M. for conspicuous gallantry at Loos, 1915.

DE'ATH, SIDNEY. School period: September, 1908, to July, 1914. Private, 2/5th Lincoln Regiment, attached 10th Garrison Battalion, King's Own Scottish Borderers. Two years. France. Invalided home.

DEAYTON, ARTHUR HARRY. School period: January, 1907, to December, 1910. Gunner, Herts. R.F.A. September, 1914, to July, 1919. France, Egypt and Palestine.

DEAYTON, GEORGE THOMAS. School period: September, 1899, to July, 1902. Corporal, R.F.A. Died of wounds received in action in the Ypres Salient, 10th August, 1917.

DEWICK, LEONARD FREDERICK. School period: September, 1912, to December, 1915. Signaller, H.A.C. One year, eight months.

DEWICK, STANLEY GULSON. School period: September, 1907, to July, 1909. Company Quarter-Master Sergeant, R.E. Four years. France.

DIGGLE, JOHN. School period: September, 1901, to December, 1905. Corporal, 102nd Battalion, Canadian Expeditionary Force. Three times wounded, St. Eloi, 1916, Passchendaele, 1917, Arras, 1918.

DODSWORTH, ARTHUR INNES. School period: September, 1912, to April, 1916. Cadet, R.F.C.

DOIG, GEORGE BEZANT. School period: September, 1911, to July, 1915. Rifleman, London Rifle Brigade.

DOLLEY, AUGUSTUS HUBERT FRANCIS. School period: September 1905, to July, 1910. R.Q.M.S., 10th Middlesex Regiment (T.F.). August, 1914, to January, 1919. India and Mesopotamia.

DOLLEY, GEOFFREY WILLIAM FRANCIS. School period: September, 1906, to September, 1909. Private, 3rd East Anglian Field Ambulance, R.A.M.C. September, 1914, to May, 1919. Dardanelles, Egypt and Palestine.

DOLLEY, LESLIE GEORGE FRANCIS. School period: September, 1907, to July, 1913. Lieutenant, 39th Battalion, Machine Gun Corps. September, 1914, to February, 1919. Enlisted in 12th London Regiment; wounded May, 1915 (second Battle of Ypres); gazetted Second Lieutenant, Worcestershire Regiment, August, 1915; transferred to Machine Gun Corps, October, 1918.

DOLLEY, REGINALD CHARLES FRANCIS. School period: September, 1901, to July, 1905. Second Lieutenant, Sherwood Foresters. Enlisted in Inns of Court O.T.C., November, 1915, and became Sergeant; gazetted to Sherwood Foresters in February, 1917; went to France; reported missing near Lens, 1st July, 1917, and since presumed killed.

DOLLEYMORE, RONALD STUART. School period: May, 1897, to July, 1902. Second Lieutenant, A.S.C.

DOWNER, ARTHUR. School period: May, 1886, to December, 1893. 1st Air Mechanic, R.F.C. November, 1916, to January, 1919.

DOWNER, EDWARD. School period: January, 1885, to May, 1893. Lieutenant, R.F.C. and R.A.F. Two years.

DREWETT, FRANK. School period: September, 1907, to July, 1909. Lance-Corporal, Machine Gun Section, 3rd Bedfordshire Regiment. September, 1914, to January, 1919.

DUDLEY, NOEL MONTAGU CHARLES. School period: January, 1906, to July, 1911. Second Lieutenant, 5th King's Liverpool Regiment. Died of wounds received at High Wood, October, 1916.

DUNBAR, LEWIS FRASER. School period: January, 1909, to July, 1911. Corporal, R.A.F.

DUNHAM, HARRY QUENBY. School period: September, 1902, to July, 1904. Private, 4th Royal Berkshire Regiment.

DUNN, FRANCIS WILLIAM. School period: April, 1902, to April, 1908. Private, 2nd Herts. Regiment.

EAMES, KENNETH DANIEL. School period: September, 1910, to July, 1917. Wireless Operator, R.A.F. 1918 to 1919.

EAMES, PERCY CHARLES. School period: September, 1905, to December, 1906. Private, Herts. Regiment.

EARLAND, ARTHUR VIVIAN. School period: February, 1904, to April, 1910. Signaller, Ceylon Planters' Rifle Corps, Ceylon Defence Force. Enlisted, October, 1914.

EAST, BENJAMIN. School period: January, 1904, to December, 1905. Sergeant, 1st Grenadier Guards. Wounded in action, 29th October, and died in a German hospital, 31st October, 1914.

EDEN, HENRY. School period: April, 1895, to March, 1900. Gunner, 2nd Herts. Battery, R.F.A.

EDSALL, VALENTINE KEITH KENDALL. School period: February, 1912, to December, 1914. Signaller, 10th Queen's Royal West Surrey Regiment. February, 1917, to February, 1919.

ELDRED, HUBERT REGINALD. School period: September, 1907, to July 1908. Sergeant, R.F.C. and R.A.F. Three years, six months. France.

ELLINGHAM, VICTOR EDWARD. School period: September, 1899, to April, 1903. Lieutenant, 9th Leicestershire Regiment. Went to France in April, 1915; wounded at Loos in September, 1916; invalided home, and went out again in following April; killed by a sniper, 22nd October, 1917.

EVANS, GEORGE WHITE. School period: September, 1907, to October, 1910. Corporal, 1st Herts. Regiment. Joined up 7th June, 1915, and went to the front in July, 1916; wounded in November, 1916, and invalided home, returning to France in September, 1917; took part in the "great push" of March, 1918, and was posted as missing on 23rd March; it was afterwards learnt that he had been buried by the Germans on or about that date.

FARLEY, EDWARD. School period: September, 1909, to July, 1913. Sergeant-Observer, R.A.F. May, 1916, to March, 1919. Awarded Medaille Militaire by French Government "for valuable services rendered."

FAYERS, SIDNEY. School period: September, 1908, to June, 1913. Corporal, 3/1st City of London Yeomanry. Awarded M.M. "for distinguished service in the field." Killed in action, 25th March, 1918.

FERRETT, ARTHUR FREDERICK. School period: April, 1900, to July, 1908. Sergeant, R.E. Four years. France and Belgium.

FEASEY, GORDON LEONARD. School period: September, 1911, to November, 1914. 2nd Air Mechanic, R.F.C. Three years. France.

FILBEE, FRANCIS WILLIAM. School period: September, 1900, to July, 1903. Regimental Sergeant-Major, 3rd County of London (Sharpshooters) Yeomanry. August, 1914, to February, 1919.

FISHER, EDMUND. Member of the Staff: September, 1914, to July, 1915. Sergeant, South Staffs. Regiment.

FLATT, DOUGLAS ARTHUR. School period: January, 1906, to July, 1908. R.A.M.C. Killed in France.

FLATT, FREDERICK WASHINGTON. School period: September, 1899, to July, 1901. R.G.A.

FLETCHER, GEORGE TREVELLIAN. School period: September, 1900, to July, 1901. Lieutenant, Army Pay Department. Four years, three months. France.

FORDHAM, ALEXANDER WILLIAM. School period: January, 1911, to December, 1912. Private, Canadians.

FORSTER, HAROLD PERCY. School period: September, 1906, to December, 1909. Trooper, Herts. Yeomanry.

FORSTER, LESLIE CLIVE. School period: January, 1907, to December, 1913. Royal Bucks. Hussars.

FORTNUM, HERBERT GEORGE. School period: September, 1909, to July, 1912. Sergeant, 4th Royal Sussex Regiment. Four years.

FOWLER, EDWARD ALEXANDER. School period: September, 1906, to June, 1910. Rifleman, Queen's Westminster Rifles. January, 1915, to March, 1919. France, Salonica and Palestine.

FOWLER, FREDERICK ALEXANDER. School period: September, 1904, to July, 1908. Signaller, H.A.C. (R.H.A.). One year.

FOX, ROBERT WILLIAM. School period: January, 1903, to April, 1908. Lieutenant, 2/7th Manchester Regiment. August, 1914, to March, 1919. Egypt, Gallipoli, France and Belgium. Wounded.

FRANKLIN, ARTHUR. School period: April, 1902, to December, 1907. Staff-Sergeant, 1st Canadian Mounted Rifles; Canadian Army Pay Corps. Four years, six months.

FRANKLIN, FREDERICK EDWARD. School period: January, 1912, to December, 1913. Private, Royal West Kent Regiment. France. Died of wounds, 30th September, 1918.

FRANKLIN, HAROLD WALTER. School period: September, 1906, to July, 1915. Corporal, R.A.F., transferred from R.N.A.S. Two years, eight months. Mediterranean.

FRANKLIN, REGINALD HECTOR. School period: January, 1904, to July, 1905. Lieutenant, 4th Essex Regiment. August, 1914, to February, 1919. France. Mentioned in despatches, December, 1917.

FRANKLIN, SIDNEY STUART. School period: January, 1904, to April, 1907. Captain and Adjutant, Queen Victoria's Rifles. August, 1914, to March, 1919. France. Mentioned in despatches, December, 1918.

FRANKLIN, VICTOR. School period: September, 1907, to April, 1912. Lance-Corporal, London Rifle Brigade, May, 1916, to February, 1918; A.S.C. (M.T.), February, 1918, to September, 1919.

FRAZER, HARRY. School period: September, 1905, to February, 1909. Black Watch.

FRAZER, SIDNEY FRANK. School period: September, 1909, to July, 1912. R.F.C.

FREAK, LESLIE ASHFIELD. School period: October, 1900, to July, 1905. Lieutenant, R.E. March, 1915, to June, 1919.

FREEMAN, HENRY ARTHUR. School period: September, 1899, to April, 1901. 1st Class Air Mechanic, R.N.A.S.

FRENCH, CLARENCE JAMES. School period: September, 1908, to February, 1913. Second Lieutenant, R.A.F. Four years. France. While Corporal in R.F.C. awarded D.C.M. "for conspicuous gallantry and devotion to duty on many occasions when the vicinity of his wireless mast was heavily shelled."

FRIEND, JOHN ALBERT NEWTON. Member of the Staff: September, 1903, to July, 1906. Captain, R.E. (Anti-Gas Dept.). May, 1916, to January, 1919.

FULKS, EDGAR CHARLES. School period: September, 1907, to April, 1911. Sergeant, 1st Herts. Regiment. Four years, six months. Wounded at Loos, October, 1915.

GALE, CYRIL JOHN HENRY. School period: September, 1907, to October, 1918. Naval Cadet, R.N.

GARDINER, ARNOLD TREVOR. School period: January, 1892, to May, 1893. Acting-Sergeant, Divisional Headquarters. Mentioned in despatches, 1917.

GARTLAND, WILLIAM LAWRENCE. School period: September, 1902, to December, 1908. Lance-Corporal, 1st London Div. Engineers.

GEORGE, FREDERICK GORDON. School period: April, 1898, to December, 1900. Rifleman, London Rifle Brigade.

GIBBS, VICTOR ROY. School period: May, 1910, to April, 1912. Second Lieutenant, 4th Gordon Highlanders. 1914 to 1919. France.

GIDDINS, STANLEY CLYTON CHAFFEY. School period: September, 1914, to March, 1915. R.F.C.

GILL, PEVENSEY ARTHUR. School period: January, 1910, to December, 1915. Private, London Scottish.

GLADWELL, ALAN MAURICE. School period: September, 1909, to April, 1912. Second Lieutenant, R.F.A.

GLADWELL, SIDNEY BERNARD. School period: September, 1907, to April, 1910. Sergeant Instructor, Army Cycle Corps.

GLEN, DAVID CORSE. School period: September, 1908, to June, 1910. Lieutenant, 8th Royal Berkshire Regiment. Killed in action in France, 25th September, 1915.

GOADBY, FREDERICK MAURICE. January, 1888, to July, 1892. Captain, Camel Transport Corps. July, 1916, to March, 1918.

GOADBY, HUGH CLIFTON. School period: April, 1907, to April, 1912. Private, Civil Service Rifles.

GOADBY, JOHN CLIFTON. School period: March, 1906, to April, 1911. Second Lieutenant, 13th London Regiment. Killed in action, 28th August, 1918; had been recommended for M.C.

GOODALL, JOHN. School period: September, 1908, to July, 1911. Private, London Scottish. Enlisted March, 1915; wounded and taken prisoner at Gommecourt, 1st July, 1916; repatriated November, 1918.

GOODMAN, GILBERT NEVILLE. Member of the Staff since September, 1915. Lieutenant, Worcestershire Regiment. Three years. India.

GOODSON, DUDLEY. School period: April, 1913, to February, 1914. Cadet, R.F.C.

GOODSON, HORACE. School period: September, 1902, to July, 1907. R.F.A.

GOSLING, GILBERT THOMAS. School period: September, 1908, to July, 1911. Lance-Corporal, R.E., Fortress Electric Light Company. November, 1915, to January, 1919.

GOSS, EDWARD OLIVER. School period: September, 1905, to July, 1909. Second Lieutenant, Royal West Surrey Regiment (The Queen's). Mobilised with Civil Service Rifles, 4th August, 1914; after seeing active service in France, returned to England for commission in February, 1917; gazetted to the Queen's and went to Italy, afterwards returning to France; died of wounds received in action, 14th October, 1918.

GOUGH, HUGH ASHWIN. School period: January, 1910, to December, 1911.

GRAHAM, ROBERT RAMAGE. School period: September, 1905, to July, 1912. Second Lieutenant, Tank Corps. One year, six months.

GRAHAM, THOMAS DONALD. School period: November, 1899, to July, 1901. Trooper, Australian Light Horse.

GRANT, STANLEY DE VERE. School period: January, 1902, to July, 1905. Lance-Corporal, King's Royal Rifles.

GRAY, ALBERT CLARENCE. School period: September, 1892, to December, 1895. Herts. Regiment.

GRAY, ARTHUR JOHN. School period: September, 1909, to July, 1916. Private, R.A.F.

GRAY, ALFRED LESLIE. School period: June, 1902, to December, 1908. Lieutenant, Inns of Court O.T.C., September, 1915; Notts. and Derby Regiment (Sherwood Foresters); wounded in France, 1917; attached 2/90th Punjabis, India, August, 1918, to October, 1919.

GRAY, GEORGE ALAN. School period: May, 1905, to July, 1912. Private, 1st Herts. Regiment. France, 1915; India, 1917.

GRAY, GEOFFREY HARRY. School period: September, 1907, to March, 1915. Lance-Corporal, 53rd Royal Sussex Regiment.

GREEN, HAROLD THORNTON. School period: September, 1905, to December, 1907. Lieutenant, 128th Pioneers (Indian Army). Enlisted in Queen's Regiment, August, 1914; Mesopotamia, 1915 to 1916; N.W. Frontier, India, 1916 to 1917.

GREENWAY, REGINALD LESLIE. School period: September, 1911, to July, 1914. Signaller, Machine Gun Corps. Enlisted as Rifleman in London Rifle Brigade. France. Two years, three months.

GREENWOOD, HENRY THOMAS. School period: September, 1911, to July, 1912. Private, Royal Sussex Regiment. Killed in action near Ypres, 26th September, 1917.

GREGORY, HERBERT LEONARD. School period: January, 1904, to July, 1907. Second Lieutenant, Middlesex Regiment. Three years, six months.

GREGORY, SIDNEY WALTER JAMES. School period: September, 1907, to July, 1910. Lieutenant, R.G.A. Four years, three months.

GRIFFIN, ARTHUR LIONEL. School period: September, 1909, to July, 1912. Rifleman, Queen's Westminster Rifles. Wounded in France, 22nd July, 1917; transferred to R.A.F. Aircraftsman, 1st class. Four years.

GRIFFIN, NEVILLE. School period: March, 1905, to December, 1908. Rifleman, Queen's Westminster Rifles. Killed in action in France, 11th October, 1915.

GRIMES, ARCHIBALD ANDREW. School period: March, 1906, to July, 1912. Private, 11th Reserve Canadian Expeditionary Force.

GRIMES, DOUGLAS FREDERICK. School period: October, 1905, to July, 1909. Corporal, R.A.O.C. August, 1914, to March, 1919. France.

GRIMES, PERCIVAL SYDNEY. School period: March, 1906, to July, 1907. Corporal, Canadian Forestry Battalion. Killed in a train accident in France, 29th January, 1918.

GROVE, LIONEL SMART. School period: September, 1909, to December, 1912. Private, 15th Royal Welsh Fusiliers. Killed in action at Fromelles, 8th May, 1916.

GYLEE, CYRIL HARCOURT. School period: September, 1909, to July, 1915. Corporal (Wireless Operator), R.F.C., attached 107th Brigade, R.F.A. Three years. France and Belgium.

HAINES, LAURENCE EDGAR. School period: September, 1906, to July, 1910. Private, R.A.M.C. Two years.

HALL, HAROLD HEDLEY BENWELL. School period: September, 1910, to July, 1915. Lance-Corporal, 9th County of London (Q.V.R.). Two years, three months.

HALSEY, ERIC CHARLES. School period: September, 1908, to July, 1913. Second Lieutenant, 7th London Regiment. Two years. France. Killed in action, 20th June, 1917.

HAMMETT, LEWIS REGINALD. School period: September, 1909, to March, 1916. Private, 2/2nd City of London Regiment (Royal Fusiliers). 1917 to 1919. Wounded in France.

HAMPTON, FREDERICK. School period: April, 1888, to July, 1894. Lance-Corporal, A.V.C. March, 1915 to 1919. Dardanelles, Egypt, France, and Italy.

HANCOCK, SIDNEY WILLIAM. School period: September, 1906, to July, 1911. Gunner, 3/4th East Anglian Brigade, R.F.A.

HANNA, JOHN HENRY. Member of the Staff, September, 1907, to December, 1912. Second Lieutenant, 19th London Regiment, attached London Rifle Brigade. Enlisted as a Private in October, 1914; wounded in France, 1916; in July, 1917, gazetted to 19th London Regiment; killed in action in the Menin Road battle, 20th September, 1917.

HARDING, FREDERICK CYRIL. School period: September, 1911, to December, 1914. Private, 2/1st Sussex Yeomanry. Two years, three months.

HARE, VICTOR FREDERICK. School period: September, 1909, to July, 1912. Inns of Court O.T.C.

HARRIS, EDWARD JAMES BURNET. School period: January, 1909, to April, 1911. Lieutenant, The Queen's Regiment. Three years. Mesopotamia and India.

HARRIS, EUSTACE CECIL. School period: September, 1907, to July, 1911. Able Seaman, R.N.V.R. Enlisted 4th August, 1914; Antwerp, October, 1914; Dardanelles; killed in action on Passchendaele Ridge, 4th November, 1917.

HARRIS, HENRY EDMUND. School period: September, 1910, to July, 1915. Second Lieutenant, The Queen's Regiment. September, 1916, to February, 1919. France. Wounded during Vimy Ridge attack, 16th April, 1917.

HARRIS, MARCUS LEWIS. School period: May, 1905, to December, 1912. Lieutenant, R.H.A. & R.F.A. Three years.

HART, STUART WILLIAM. School period: April, 1900, to December, 1905. Lance-Corporal, 21st London Regiment. Killed in action, 23rd May, 1916.

HARVEY, WALTER STEAN. School period: May, 1899, to December, 1907. Captain, King's Own Royal Lancs. Regiment. Five years. France, Egypt and Palestine. Awarded M.C. "for conspicuous gallantry and disregard of all personal danger when getting supplies and ammunition forward, and in maintaining communications during operations," 2nd March, 1916, Ypres Salient.

HAWKER, WILLIAM JAMES EDWIN. School period: May, 1904, to December, 1905. Corporal, R.A.S.C., attached R.A.M.C. March, 1915, to January, 1919. France. Awarded M.M., March, 1918.

HAWKINS, WILLIAM JAMES. School period: September, 1907, to July, 1911. Company Sergeant-Major, 23rd London Regiment. France. Awarded D.C.M. [Has since died of gas-consumption at Military Sanatorium, Ware, 15th November, 1919.]

HAYES, CHARLES WILLIAM. School period: November, 1908, to March, 1916. 1st Air Mechanic, R.A.F. One year, four months.

HAYNES, FREDERICK CHARLES GAMBLE. School period: September, 1905, to July, 1908. Second Lieutenant, 8th Seaforth Highlanders.

HAYWOOD, HARRY MAURICE. School period: April, 1898, to April, 1904. Captain and Adjutant, 3rd County of London Yeomanry (Sharpshooters); Royal Bucks. Hussars; 101st (Bucks. and Berks. Yeomanry) Battalion, Machine Gun Corps. August, 1914, to May, 1919. Egypt and Palestine with Royal Bucks. Hussars, and France and Belgium with M.G.C. Torpedoed in Mediterranean, 26-27th May, 1918.

HEATH, JOHN WINFIELD. School period: September, 1907, to July, 1913. Midshipman, H.M.S. "Conqueror."

HEATHER, JOHN CAMERON. School period: September, 1907, to July, 1913. 13th London Regiment (Kensingtons). Killed in action in France, 9th September, 1916.

HEATHER, THOMAS WILLIAM. School period: May, 1905, to December, 1910. Staff-Captain, 1st Middlesex Regiment. Awarded M.C. — "no information having been received as to the progress of the attack, this officer went forward alone to reconnoitre under heavy shell and machine-gun fire. He returned with valuable information, and having found, on his way back, a wounded officer in a shell hole, he obtained a volunteer from the Reserve Company, and brought him in safely under persistent fire from snipers." Awarded bar to M.C., 1918. Twice mentioned in despatches, June, 1917, and July, 1918.

HEATHER, WILLIAM ROBSON FRANCIS. School period: May, 1910, to November, 1915. Private, London Scottish.

HEATON, NOEL. School period: September, 1885, to July, 1891. Captain, General List, attached Headquarters, 19th Division. Five years.

HEBERT, HUGH RICARDO MELBOURNE. School period: September, 1907, to June, 1911. Lieutenant, R.A.F. Nine months. Prior to this service, joined up in September, 1914, but was invalided in January, 1915.

HEDDERWICK, ALEXANDER. School period: September, 1906, to July, 1908. Private, 1/10th Middlesex Regiment. India. Discharged as medically unfit, November, 1915.

HEDDERWICK, ROBERT SAMUEL. School period: September, 1909, to July, 1913. Rifleman, Queen's Westminster Rifles; transferred to R.A.F. in March, 1918. Three years, six months. France, Salonica, Egypt and Palestine.

HEMMING, STANLEY. School period: September, 1908, to March, 1914. Lance-Corporal, 8th Bedfordshire Regiment. Killed in attack near Loos, 19th April, 1917: had been recommended for a commission.

HESLAM, REGINALD HENRY. School period: September, 1909, to June, 1911. Trooper, Herts. Yeomanry. September, 1914, to September, 1919.

HEWLETT, WILLIAM JAMES THOMAS. School period: April, 1884, to December, 1892. Commander, Mine-Sweeper, R.N.R.

HIGGINBOTHAM, HAROLD. School period: September, 1908, to July, 1911. Gunner, R.G.A.

HILL, ARTHUR ROWLAND. School period: January, 1904, to June, 1909. Private, 13th County of London Regiment. Wounded at Aubers Ridge, 9th May, 1915, and died in hospital a few days later.

HILL, BERTRAND ERNEST. School period: May, 1905, to July, 1910. Private, 13th County of London Regiment.

HILL, FRANCIS WILLIAM. School period: March, 1899, to July, 1904. Corporal, A.V.C.

HILL, WILLIAM ERNEST. School period: September, 1912, to July, 1916. Cadet, R.A.F.

HILLS, LESLIE CONWAY. School period: May, 1905, to January, 1913. Lieutenant, Royal Marine Artillery.

HODGES, GEORGE HENRY. School period: June, 1888, to July, 1889. Trooper, Herts. Yeomanry.

HODGINS, ERNEST. School period: September, 1901, to July, 1905. Lieutenant, R.F.A. Joined Herts. Yeomanry, September, 1914. Egypt, Gallipoli and Palestine. Commissioned 1st December, 1917, India. Five years, three months.

HODGSON, DAVID CROWE. School period: September, 1906, to January, 1910. Second Lieutenant, Lincoln Regiment.

HODGSON, ROBERT NELSON. School period: September, 1910, to December, 1912. Killed in action.

HOLLINS, URBAN. School period: January, 1903, to July, 1908. Lance-Corporal, 4th Field Survey Company, R.E.

HOLMES, CHARLES NEVILLE. School period: February, 1900, to December, 1903. Machine Gun Section, 50th Canadians. Killed in France, 24th February, 1917.

HOLT, ARTHUR JOHN. School period: September, 1906, to July, 1911. Private, 2nd Herts. Regiment.

HOLT, EDWARD. School period: September, 1890, to December, 1897. Second Lieutenant, R.A.F. Served in R.A.M.C. in France and Salonica. Four years.

HOLT, ROBERT GEORGE. School period: September, 1908, to July, 1910. Private, 25th London Regiment.

HORNE, SAMUEL WILLIAM. School period: September, 1905, to July, 1909. Sapper, Special Brigade, R.E. November, 1916, to January, 1919. France, two years. Gassed at Amiens.

HORNE, WALTER ERNEST. School period: September, 1908, to July, 1909. Sergeant; Royal Fusiliers, R.E. (Wireless Section), Tank Corps. September, 1914, to April, 1919. France four years.

HORTON, EDWARD. School period: February, 1906, to December, 1909. Private, 26th Royal Fusiliers.

HORTON, THOMAS GEOFFREY. School period: September, 1905, to July, 1907. Rifleman, Queen's Westminster Rifles. Two years. France. Prisoner of war, nine months.

HOUSEHOLD, ERNEST SCOTT. School period: September, 1908, to July, 1910. Second Lieutenant, 5th Essex Regiment. Joined Inns of Court O.T.C. in November, 1915; obtained commission, 25th January, 1917. Brigade Bombing Instructor. France and Flanders. Wounded, 19th July, 1917, at Monchy-le-Preux, and died three days later.

HUMPHREY, ARTHUR HENRY. School period: January, 1903, to December, 1905. Private, Army Pay Corps.

HUNT, ERNEST ALDINGTON. School period: April, 1903, to October, 1909. Second Lieutenant, Australian Expeditionary Force. Three years, three months.

HUNT, ERNEST HERMANN. School period: September, 1905, to July, 1906. Private, 9th Middlesex Regiment.

HUNT, JOHN GILBERT PRESTON. School period: September, 1905, to July, 1908. Lieutenant, 11th Middlesex Regiment. Four years, six months. Egypt, Gallipoli and France.

HUNT, WILLIAM GILBERT. School period: January, 1906, to July, 1907. Sergeant, 7th London Regiment. Five years, nine months. Wounded at Loos, 25th September, 1915; one year and six months' service in East Africa with King's African Rifles.

HUTCHINGS, ARTHUR STANLEY. School period: September, 1896, to July, 1902. Corporal, R.A.F., transferred from R.N.A.S. February, 1916, to January, 1919.

IBBOTSON, ALLEYNE. School period: September, 1896, to December, 1903. Acting Lance-Corporal, 10th Battalion, 1st Canadians. Two years. Killed in action at Vimy Ridge, 28th April, 1917.

IBBOTSON, OWEN EDWARD. School period: April, 1900, to December, 1907. Corporal, 38th Battery, 4th Division, Australian Expeditionary Force. Four years, four months. Severely wounded in Gallipoli, slightly wounded and again severely wounded in France.

IBBOTSON, RUPERT. School period: April, 1900, to December, 1906. Private, Bedfordshire Regiment. Three years, two months. Severely wounded at second battle of Ypres, and in hospital for two years, six months.

IBBOTT, ARTHUR DAVID. School period: January, 1905, to April, 1906. Private, Loyal North Lancs. Regiment. France. Reported missing, 3rd September, 1916: presumed killed.

IBBOTT, BERTRAM CHARLES. School period: January, 1907, to July, 1912. Private, 92nd Machine Gun Corps. Wounded by a shell and died in hospital, 16th July, 1917.

INGLEBY, HUGH HERINGTON. School period: September, 1905, to December, 1912. Private, R.A.M.C.

INWOOD, WALTER SAMUEL. School period: January, 1903, to July, 1909. Lance-Corporal, 31st Royal Fusiliers. Enlisted 7th February, 1916. Killed in action on the Somme, 14th November, 1916; had been selected for a commission.

ISTERLING, FREDERICK. School period: September, 1907, to December, 1910; Lance-Corporal, R.E. (Railway Transport).

JACKMAN, WILLIAM THOMAS: School period: September, 1907, to July, 1912. Driver, R.F.A. April, 1915, to March, 1919. France and Palestine.

JACKSON, FREDERICK JAMES. School period: January, 1909, to December, 1911. Lieutenant, 27th Royal Fusiliers and 5th Durham Light Infantry. Three years. France.

JAGGARD, GEORGE WILLIAM. School period: January, 1911, to April, 1914. A.S.C. (Motor Transport).

JAMES, CYRIL WILLIAM. School period: September, 1906, to July, 1910. Second Lieutenant, Machine Gun Corps.

JAMES, HAROLD CECIL BAMFORD. School period: September, 1906, to July, 1912. Lance-Corporal, 15th King's Royal Rifles.

JAMES, HARRY RUSSELL. School period: April, 1902, to December, 1906. Captain, Royal West Kent Regiment. Five years, six months. France.

JAMES, HERBERT ARTHUR. School period: April, 1907, to December, 1908. Lance-Corporal, 5th Dorset Regiment. Enlisted August, 1914; wounded, 1st July, 1916, on the Somme and again on November 16th at Beaumont Hamel; killed in action, 22nd February, 1918.

JAMES, JOHN STUART. School period: May, 1904, to December, 1906. Lieutenant, Labour Corps. Three years, nine months. France.

JAMES, LAURENCE EDWARD. School period: September to December, 1906. Captain, The London Regiment. Joined 31st May, 1915. France. Awarded M.C. "for conspicuous bravery at Ypres," 1917.

JAMES, RALPH FREDERICK. School period: September, 1905, to July, 1910. Second Lieutenant, 5th Royal Fusiliers.

JENNINGS, WILLIAM. School period: July, 1914, to March, 1915. 3rd Air Mechanic, R.N.A.S. December, 1917, to February, 1919.

JOHN, JAMES HENRY. School period: January, 1905, to July, 1913. Captain, 3rd Leicestershire Regiment. Four years, three months. Wounded, 15th September, 1916; prisoner of war, 22nd March, 1918. France.

JOHNSON, DOUGLAS JAMES. School period: April, 1912, to July, 1914. Rifleman, London Rifle Brigade. Reported missing, 28th March, 1918, near Arras: presumed killed.

JONES, CYRIL ANSLEY. School period: January, 1903, to December, 1905. 2nd Class Air Mechanic, R.N.A.S. Died of dysentery at Himo, East Africa, 21st April, 1916.

JONES, EDWARD COLLETT. School period: September, 1911, to July, 1914. Private, East Surrey Regiment. Two years, six months.

JONES, HERBERT HENRY. School period: January, 1907, to December, 1911. A.S.C.

JONES, JOHN EDWARD. School period: September, 1897, to July, 1900. Second Lieutenant, R.F.A.

JONES, LEWIS PERCY. School period: January, 1911, to December, 1912. 2nd Writer, R.N. November, 1914, to August, 1919.

JONES, LLEWELLYN RODWELL. Member of the Staff: September, 1909, to July, 1911. Captain, 2/7th West Yorkshire Regiment.

JONES, REGINALD ARTHUR. School period: April, 1909, to December, 1911. Corporal, Bedfordshire Regiment. Four years, six months.

JUDD, FRANK. School period: September, 1906, to July, 1909. Battery Quarter-Master Sergeant, R.F.A. August, 1914, to February, 1919.

JUDD, FREDERICK GEORGE HAMBROOK. School period: April, 1896, to July, 1900. 2nd Corporal, London Electrical Engineers, R.E. (T.). May, 1916, to February, 1919.

JUDGE, SYDNEY ROBERT. School period: January, 1899, to April, 1906. Trooper, Herts. Yeomanry. Four years, six months. Awarded M.M.—"In the pursuit after the fall of Gaza a small patrol was ordered to get in touch with the Australian Cavalry. Judge returned alone to the G.O.C. with valuable information—about 15 miles in all—exposed to heavy fire most of the way," 8th November, 1917.

KEMPTON, CHARLES ROBERT. School period: April, 1896, to April, 1903. Gunner, 1st Montreal Battery, R.F.A. Served throughout the war; twice wounded. France.

KEMPTON, RALPH OSBORNE. School period: January, 1899, to April, 1907. Lance-Corporal, 87th Canadian Grenadier Guards. Two years, three months. Killed in action at Lens, 15th August, 1917.

KENNEDY, CLAUDE WYNDHAM. School period: September, 1908, to April, 1912. Private, R.A.M.C. Three years, nine months. Mesopotamia and France.

KETTLE, WILFRED. School period: January, 1902, to July, 1905. Private, 1st Herts. Regiment.

KIMPTON, FRANK. School period: September, 1902, to July, 1904. Private, 13th Battalion, Australians. Killed in action at the Dardanelles, 22nd August, 1915, after eight months' service.

KIMPTON, JOSEPH MATTHEW. School period: September, 1910, to July, 1913. Signaller, R.F.A. September, 1914, to September, 1919. Mesopotamia.

KING, FRANCIS WILLIAM. School period: September, 1912, to December, 1914. Private, 30th T.R.B.

KING, HARRY JAMES. School period: January, 1905, to April, 1906. Corporal, Middlesex Regiment. Killed in action at Arras, 9th April, 1917.

KING, HERBERT HARVEY. School period: May, 1910, to April, 1912. Corporal, C.L.B. Battalion, King's Royal Rifles. 1914 to 1919. Transferred to R.E. (Signals) in May, 1917, and served as a Despatch Rider with the 31st Signal Company (1st Indian Army Corps) in Mesopotamia and the 44th Division Signal Company on the North-West Frontier of India.

KING, SIDNEY MARTIN. School period: April, 1901, to December, 1906. Rifleman, King's Royal Rifles. 1914 to March, 1917. Discharged, owing to wounds received in France.

KING, THOMAS EDWARD. School period: April to July, 1909. Private, Hampshire Regiment. Two years, three months.

KINGHAM, WILLIAM RANDOLPH. School period: January, 1900, to July, 1903. Member of the Staff: September, 1912, to January, 1919. Gunner, H.A.C. Siege Battery. April, 1917, to January, 1919. France.

KIRKLAND, CLARK MILLER. School period: September, 1913, to July, 1917. Private, 26th Royal Fusiliers. One year, six months.

KIRKMAN, ALFRED HENRY WILBURN. School period: September, 1905, to July, 1908. Company Sergeant-Major, Intelligence Corps. November, 1915, to March, 1919. 9th and 21st Lancers till February, 1917. France. Awarded M.S.M.

KNAPPETT, ARTHUR ROY. School period: April, 1909, to July, 1915. Second Lieutenant, Middlesex Regiment. One year, three months.

KNOWLES, VICTOR FRANCIS. School period: September, 1909, to July, 1911. Private, 1st London Regiment.

LAMB, ROBERT JOHN. School period: September, 1912, to July, 1915. 2nd Class Mechanic, R.N., transferred from R.N.A.S. One year, four months.

LANGDON, CHARLES OSMOND. School period: September, 1900, to December, 1904. Private, 13th London Regiment. Four years, six months.

LANGDON, HUGH ALBERT. School period: September, 1900, to December, 1904. Sergeant, R.G.A. Three years, six months.

LANSLEY, JOHN. School period: April, 1896, to July, 1901. Lieutenant and Adjutant, commanding Southern Command Labour Centre. Signal Sergeant, 6th Royal Warwickshire Regiment, 1914 to 1917. Five years, six months.

LANSLEY, SIDNEY. School period: April, 1901, to May, 1904. Lieutenant, 21st London Regiment (1st Surrey Rifles). Five years.

LARRETT, WALTER DENHAM. School period: September, 1911, to May, 1916. Corporal, Army Pay Corps. February, 1918, to October, 1919.

LAURIE, ROBERT CHARLES MICHAEL. School period: September, 1913, to February, 1916. Cadet, R.F.C.

LEADER, EDWARD CHARLES. School period: September, 1910, to July, 1914. Private, Coldstream Guards. Nine months. Invalided, August, 1917.

LEDGER, CHARLES. School period: September, 1911, to July, 1914. Corporal (Machine Gun Instructor), 17th Lancashire Fusiliers. Two years. France.

LEDGER, HAROLD GEORGE. School period: September, 1909, to July, 1912. Lieutenant, Oxford and Bucks. Light Infantry. November, 1915, to March, 1919. Artists' Rifles O.T.C. till September, 1916; prisoner of war, March to November, 1918.

LEES, BERNARD GEORGE. School period: April, 1906, to April, 1914. Private, London Scottish.

LEES, SYDNEY CHARLES. School period: April, 1902, to April, 1910. Private, London Scottish. Killed in action in France, 29th September, 1915.

LEES, SYDNEY GEORGE. School period: January to July, 1908. Private, R.A.M.C. August, 1914, to May, 1919.

LEWIS, ALBERT VICTOR. School period: September, 1908, to April, 1911. Lance-Corporal, 6th Royal Sussex Cycle Corps. Four years. For two years in 1st Garrison Battalion, Somerset Light Infantry. India.

LEWIS, HENRY FRANCIS. School period: September, 1912, to April, 1916. Marconi Operator, Mercantile Marine. One year, six months.

LINNELL, CHARLES GORDON. School period: January, 1904, to April, 1906.

LITTLE, CHARLES GEORGE. School period: May, 1910, to July, 1914. Private, Army Ordnance Corps, October, 1916, to May, 1917; Machine Gun Corps, May, 1917, to November, 1919. wounded at Maricourt, 23rd March, 1918.

LLOYD, EDWARD COWEN CLIFFORD. School period: April, 1903, to December, 1910. Corporal, 54th Divisional Artillery, H.Q. Staff. Five years.

LLOYD, HENRY GORDON. School period: September, 1908, to July, 1913. Private, 6th Northamptonshire Regiment. Two years. Awarded M.M. "for bravery and devotion to duty" at Preux, 4th November, 1918.

LOFTS, BERNARD. School period: October, 1900, to July, 1903. Private, 6th Royal Scots. Went to France, October, 1914. Killed in action at Festubert, 16th May, 1915.

LOFTS, FRANK. School period: January, 1902, to April, 1907. Lieutenant, 4th Middlesex Regiment. Wounded at Beaucourt during the Ancre Battle, November, 1916.

LOFTS, NORMAN. School period: January, 1905, to December, 1907. Rifleman (Prince Consort's Own) Rifle Brigade. France. Taken prisoner near St. Quentin, 21st March, 1918.

LOFTS, WILFRED. School period: September, 1905, to December, 1914. Second Lieutenant, R.A.F. (48th Squadron). Joined Royal Fusiliers in June, 1916; obtained commission in R.A.F. in spring of 1918. Killed in action in France, 9th August, 1918.

LONGTHORNE, WILLIAM GERALD. School period: May, 1904, to April, 1906. Regimental Sergeant-Major, 1st Herts. Regiment. Four years, seven months. France. Awarded M.M., 1916, D.C.M., March, 1918.

LUDBROOK, JOHN WALLIS. School period: May, 1899, to July, 1905. Signalman, R.N.V.R. Two years, six months. North Sea.

LUMM, GEORGE. School period: September, 1905, to July, 1909. R.E.

MACKLEY, SIDNEY GEORGE. School period: September, 1911, to November, 1915. W/T Observer, R.A.F. Two years. Anti-Submarine Patrol, English Channel, North Russia.

MAILE, JOHN WILLIAM KINGSLEY. School period: April, 1907, to July, 1909. Sergeant, R.E. (London Electrical Engineers). August, 1914, to January, 1919. Coast Defence.

MAINWOOD, HAROLD. School period: September, 1906, to July, 1911. Private, 10th Middlesex Regiment.

MAJOR, REGINALD FREDERICK. School period: September, 1912, to July, 1915. Private, 33rd Machine Gun Corps. Wounded 24th June, 1918.

MANSFIELD, HUGH LLOYD. School period: September, 1912, to December, 1915. Air Mechanic, R.A.F. Joined in February, 1918. North-West Frontier of India.

MANTON, GRENVILLE GORDON OLIVER. School period: September, 1912, to July, 1915. Lieutenant, R.F.C. Two years, six months.

MARLER, EDWARD GEORGE. School period: September, 1911, to March, 1915. Wireless Operator, Indian Marine. December, 1916, to November, 1918. Atlantic Ocean, Mediterranean and Persian Gulf.

MARSHALL, ALBERT EDWARD. School period: April, 1909, to December, 1911. R.A.M.C.

MARSHALL, WILLIAM. School period: September, 1902, to July, 1909. Lieutenant, Royal Welsh Fusiliers. Four years, three months. Egypt and Palestine.

MARTIN, ALDERSON LESLIE ATKIN. School period: September, 1911, to April, 1914. Corporal, R.E. North Russia. Awarded Silver Medal for Gallantry (to be worn with ribbon of Order of St. Stanislav) by Provisional North Russian Government.

MASSER, ALFRED HENRY. School period: September, 1912, to December, 1916. 1st British Ambulance for Italy. December, 1916, to July, 1917.

MASTERS, NORMAN EDWARD JAMES. School period: January, 1907, to July, 1910. Trooper, 1st King Edward's Horse. Four years. France for three years, four months; finally at R.A.F. Cadet School.

MATHER, JOHN. School period: May, 1903, to February, 1908. Warrant Officer (Wireless), R.N.R. August, 1914, to February, 1919. West and East Africa, North Sea and Northern Russia.

MAYES, HARRY HARRIS. School period: March, 1901, to December, 1907. Staff-Sergeant, 75th Motor Transport Company, A.S.C.

McCUBBIN, LESLIE EWART. School period: September, 1912, to July, 1916. Private, 51st Middlesex Regiment. Six months.

MIDDLETON, CYRIL WOODBOURNE. School period: September, 1909, to December, 1914. Second Lieutenant, The Buffs.

MIDDLETON, HECTOR ROWLAND. School period: September, 1912, to July, 1918. Private, Inns of Court O.T.C.

MILLS, ROGER CHARLES EDWARD. School period: June, 1899, to July, 1902. Sergeant, 1/3rd City of London Yeomanry.

MING, WILLIAM JAMES. School period: September, 1909, to July, 1914. Private, A.S.C. (M.T.). Three years.

MITCHINSON, GEORGE ERNEST. School period: September, 1893, to December, 1898. Corporal, R.A.M.C. December, 1914, to November, 1919. Mesopotamia (three years), India and Egypt.

MOFFET, JOHN LEESON. School period: September, 1896, to July, 1903. Second Lieutenant, 3rd (attached 2nd) Royal Scots Fusiliers. Enlisted August, 1914; killed in action at Neuve Chapelle, 10th March, 1915.

MOFFET, THOMAS ARTHUR. School period: September, 1901, to July, 1905. Major, 10th Scottish Battalion, King's Liverpool Regiment. Enlisted August, 1914.

MOORE, SIDNEY. School period: March, 1907, to July, 1909. Rifleman, King's Royal Rifles.

MOORHOUSE, JOHN RICHARD. School period: September, 1911, to December, 1913. Second Lieutenant, R.F.C. September, 1917, to April, 1919. Awarded D.F.C.

MORETON, TOM. School period: September, 1913, to March, 1916. Observer, R.A.F. Two years, six months.

MORLEY, HERBERT ALFRED. School period: October, 1900, to July, 1905. Second Lieutenant, R.A.F. Three years, seven months.

MORRIS, SIDNEY RUPERT OWEN. School period: September, 1906, to July, 1909. Sergeant, Machine Gun Corps. August, 1914, to December, 1919. Wounded at Guedecourt on the Somme, 1916.

MORSE, HAROLD EWART. School period: April, 1902, to July, 1909. Sergeant, 1st Herts. Regiment, transferred to Gloucester Regiment. Enlisted August, 1914; wounded at La Bassée, 14th February, 1915; killed in action in France, 18th November, 1916; awarded M.M.—"On 22nd and 23rd July, 1916, when his Officer and Sergeant had become casualties, Lance-Corporal Morse took charge of a carrying party of 25 men and reorganised them under heavy shell fire. He made three journeys with ammunition through the enemy barrage along a road where all units had suffered heavy casualties."

MORTON, FREDERICK WILLIAM. School period: April, 1902, to July, 1905. Lieutenant, London Rifle Brigade, 10th London Regiment, and 175th Trench Mortar Battery. Two years, six months. Awarded M.C.—"On 22nd September, 1918, near Epehy, while in charge of two Stokes guns, he engaged and killed twenty-five of the enemy who had pushed forward to avoid our bombardment of their posts. During an attack the same night he completely silenced three hostile machine guns. After consolidation he got forward large supplies of ammunition and effectively engaged numerous targets. His courage and dash set a fine example to his men."

MOYES, MAURICE EDWARD. School period: September, 1909, to April, 1913. Corporal, 29th Middlesex Regiment, transferred to A.S.C. (Remounts). Egypt.

NASH, FRANK BRANCH. School period: September, 1907, to December, 1910. Rifleman, 9th London Regiment (Queen Victoria's Rifles). Enlisted in November, 1914; reported missing, 1st July, 1916: presumed killed.

NASH, JOHN HALLETT. School period: September, 1909, to July, 1913. Signaller, 3rd Royal West Kent Regiment.

NASH, THOMAS. School period: September, 1907, to September, 1908. C.Q.M.S., 13th Rifle Brigade. September, 1914, to March, 1919. Wounded at Beaucourt, 14th November, 1916.

NASH, WILFRED BRANCH. School period: May, 1910, to July, 1911. Lance-Corporal, 13th Rifle Brigade. 1917 to 1919.

NASH, WILLIAM EDWARD. School period: September, 1910, to July, 1915. Signaller, 1st Artists' Rifles.

NAYLER, ROBERT HENRY AMOS. School period: September, 1912, to July, 1915. Second Lieutenant, R.F.C.

NAYLOR, ALEXANDER JOHN. School period: January, 1912, to April, 1914. R.F.C.

NEAL, WILLIAM JOHN. School period: April, 1884, to July, 1886. Lieutenant, King's African Rifles. Four years, six months.

NEATE, CYRIL FRANK CÆSAR. School period: April, 1906, to July, 1911. Sub-Lieutenant, R.N. Joined 12th April, 1917.

NEWCOMBE, FREDERICK GEORGE. Member of the Staff since September, 1908. Lieutenant, R.G.A. January, 1916, to January, 1919. France. Awarded M.C.—"when in charge of a party getting two guns into a new position, he carried out the work successfully, under very heavy shell fire, although more than half of his party became casualties," 1917.

NEWMAN, FRANK EDWARD. School period: January, 1897, to December, 1899. R.F.C.

NEWTON, HOWARD FRANK. School period: September, 1910, to June, 1913. Private, King's Shropshire Light Infantry. November, 1915, to March, 1919.

NICHOLSON, ARTHUR JAMES. School period: September, 1899, to April, 1903. Lieutenant, R.F.A. August, 1914, to June, 1919. France, Egypt and Palestine.

NICHOLSON, DOUGLAS WALTER JAMES. School period: September, 1910, to July, 1914. Private, Acting-Sergeant Cadet, R.A.F., transferred from R.N.A.S. November, 1917, to February, 1919.

NORMAN, EDMUND GOLLIDGE. School period: January, 1892, to July, 1898. Second Lieutenant, 19th Sherwood Foresters.

NORMAN, ROBERT AUGUSTUS. School period: January, 1892, to February, 1895. Second Lieutenant, R.A.M.C.

NORMAN, SIGARD OSWALD. School period: September, 1909, to July, 1911. Captain, 12th Battalion Tank Corps. Four years, six months. Awarded M.C.—"For conspicuous gallantry and devotion to duty. He fought his tank with the greatest skill and energy, locating and silencing several enemy machine guns and later, unsupported, he passed through the enemy lines and dealt with many targets."

NORTH, WILLIAM JAMES. School period: January, 1913, to July, 1915. Air Mechanic, R.A.F. Ten months.

NORTON, REGINALD ARTHUR. School period: May, 1910, to December, 1915. Cadet, Inns of Court O.T.C. Rifleman, King's Royal Rifle Corps. One year, three months.

ODAMS, RONALD CHARLIE. School period: September, 1910, to February, 1917. London Electrical Engineers (R.E.). February, 1917, to December, 1918.

OSBORN, CECIL HENRY. School period: January, 1904, to July, 1911. Private, 5th Royal Sussex Regiment. Killed in action, April, 1918.

OSBORN, STANLEY EDWARD CHARLES. School period: January, 1904, to April, 1910. Rifleman, 2nd Rifle Brigade.

OWEN, FRANCIS ERNEST. School period: September, 1909, to December, 1914. 2nd Air Mechanic, R.N.A.S.

OXLEY, ALAN RICE. School period: January, 1908, to July, 1914. Captain, R.A.F. France and Italy. Wounded, 1916. Awarded D.F.C., July, 1918, on Italian Front—"In company with another officer, attacked enemy formation of fifteen planes and destroyed two of them; repeatedly attacked the remaining thirteen with the result that six were destroyed and one driven out of control; two days later destroyed two more enemy aircraft."

OXLEY, FREDERICK WILLIAM HALL. School period: April, 1898, to July, 1901. Second Lieutenant, R.F.C. Italy.

OXLEY, GEORGE KENNETH RICE. School period: January, 1908, to December, 1914. Lieutenant, R.A.F. Inns of Court O.T.C., 24th December, 1914; A.S.C., R.F.C. and R.A.F. France, Salonica and Egypt. Torpedoed in Mediterranean, 1917.

PAGE, ARTHUR VALENTINE. School period: January, 1900, to July, 1903. Second Lieutenant.

PALLETT, EDWIN. School period: September, 1910, to July, 1912. Sergeant, R.E. Four years, six months. Gallipoli, Egypt and France. Mentioned in despatches.

PALMER, ALGEY. School period: September, 1900, to July, 1901. Lieutenant (Temp. Captain), 1/6th Northumberland Fusiliers. Awarded D.S.O. in North Russia, March, 1919—"This officer showed magnificent courage and great ability during the attacks on Vistafka, February 28th—March 4th, 1919. During very heavy shelling and machine-gun fire, he stood on the roof of a house observing our artillery fire and by his accurate and prompt reports rendered invaluable services. His whole work during over a month's unrelieved service in the front line has been very fine."

PALMER, EDWARD LEOPOLD. School period: September, 1906, to December, 1909. Lieutenant, 1st Lincolnshire Regiment. Three years, six months. France.

PALMER, REGINALD JOHN. School period: September, 1906, to July, 1907. Lieutenant, 2nd Northants. Regiment. Four years, eleven months. France.

PANTER, KENNETH HARRY. School period: September, 1908, to April, 1913. 2nd Corporal, R.E., transferred from Essex Regiment. Three years. France.

PARKER, ALEC BERTRAM. School period: September, 1912, to December, 1914. Writer (First Class), R.N.

PARKER, HORACE FRANK. School period: September, 1909, to April, 1912. Lieutenant, Tank Corps. Enlisted in Royal Fusiliers, 1914. Egypt, France.

PARKES, FREDERIC. School period: September, 1904, to July, 1912. Private, Civil Service Rifles. One year. Reported missing, 15th September, 1916, in Somme battle: presumed killed.

PARKES, RICHARD LIONEL. School period: January, 1906, to December, 1912. Second Lieutenant, 9th Royal Fusiliers. Two years, two months. Killed in action in France, 7th October, 1916.

PARRIS, GILBERT FRANK. School period: September, 1906, to July, 1910. Private, 2nd South Midland Mounted Field Ambulance, R.A.M.C.(T.). Four years. Gallipoli, Egypt and Palestine. Transferred to 1/5th Essex Regiment in June, 1918.

PATERSON, DUNCAN ALEXANDER. School period: April, 1909, to December, 1914. Acting-Sergeant, R.F.C. One year, three months.

PATERSON, FRANK JAMES. School period: September, 1911, to December, 1913. Second Lieutenant, 2/4th London Regiment. Awarded M.C.—"for conspicuous gallantry and dashing leadership at Peizière on 10th September, 1918."

PATERSON, ROBERT. School period: April, 1909, to July, 1911. Rifleman, 16th London Regiment.

PATTERSON, FRANCIS HALL. School period: September, 1905, to July, 1913. Lance-Corporal, Machine Gun Corps. Five years.

PAYNE, REGINALD WAKEFIELD. School period: May, 1904, to July, 1912. Corporal (Acting Battalion Bombing Instructor), 2/5th The Buffs and 1/24th London Regiment (The Queen's). Three years, six months. France, two years; returned to England to join Cadet School.

PEAR, GEORGE. School period: September, 1908, to July, 1911. Trooper, 1/1st Herts. Yeomanry. October, 1915, to March, 1919. France, Egypt, Palestine and Syria.

PEAT, DAVID MEALLS. School period: September, 1909, to December, 1910. C.Q.M.S., Seaforth Highlanders. September, 1914, to June, 1919.

PEMBERTON, BASIL. School period: September, 1897, to July, 1902. Lieutenant, R.N.V.R., Mine Clearing Service. December, 1915, to April, 1919.

PEMBERTON, LEIGH. School period: September, 1907, to July, 1914. Second Lieutenant, 9th King's Royal Rifles. One year, one month. Killed in action at Loos, 26th September, 1915.

PHILLIPS, FREDERICK GEORGE. School period: April, 1902, to July, 1908. Sergeant, 1st Herts. Regiment. September, 1914, to February, 1919. Awarded M.M.—"for gallantry and devotion to duty in the attack on St. Julien," 1917.

PHILLIPS, REGINALD. School period: September, 1904, to February, 1911. Corporal, 1st Herts. Regiment. September, 1914, to March, 1919. Wounded in France.

PINN, TYRELL STEVENTON. School period: September, 1893, to July, 1896. Second Lieutenant, 8th East Yorkshire Regiment. Died of wounds at Rouen, 12th October, 1915.

PITKIN, ARTHUR. School period: September, 1908, to April, 1911. 2nd Herts. Battery, R.F.A.

PITKIN, HENRY. School period: September, 1905, to July, 1909. 2nd Herts. Battery, R.F.A.

PONTON, ALFRED GEORGE GODMAN. School period: September, 1911, to March, 1915. Trooper, King Edward's Horse.

POPE, BERNARD CHARLES. School period: January, 1898, to December, 1899. Private, A.S.C. (Railway Transport).

PORT, FREDERICK JOHN. School period: September, 1897, to September, 1900. Staff-Captain, R.A. December, 1915, to February, 1919. France.

PORTER, HUBERT GREGORY. School period: September, 1908, to July, 1915. Private, H.A.C. One year, six months. Invalided out in November, 1919.

POSNER, PHILIP ERNEST. School period: April, 1909, to July, 1914. Second Lieutenant, 3rd South Staffordshire Regiment, attached 8th Lincolns. Wounded 28th April, 1917, and reported missing, presumed killed; recommended for M.C.

PREWETT, BERTRAM. School period: June, 1886, to July, 1894. Rifleman, London Rifle Brigade. Joined up in March, 1915; went to France, January, 1917; killed in action at Bouchavesnes, 31st August, 1918.

PRICHARD, ARTHUR HEAWORD. School period: May, 1886, to July, 1892.

PRIME, ERNEST FRANK. School period: January, 1911, to April, 1912. Private, Coldstream Guards.

PROCTER, GEORĞE ERIC. School period: January, 1907, to July, 1911. Lieutenant, R.G.A. March, 1915, to December, 1918. France.

PULMAN, FREDERICK HENRY JAMES. School period: September, 1906, to July, 1911. Lance-Corporal, 1/10th Middlesex Regiment. August, 1914, to March, 1919. India.

PUSEY, HAROLD JOHN. School period: March, 1897, to April, 1900. Trooper, 1st Herts. Yeomanry.

PUSEY, HERBERT JAMES. School period: April, 1895, to December, 1896. Second Lieutenant, A.S.C. (Transport).

QUESNEY, HENRI. School period: October, 1903, to July, 1904. Sergeant, 231st French Infantry Brigade.

RAE, JAMES ALBERT. School period: September, 1909, to June, 1910. Second Lieutenant, Cambridgeshire Regiment. Killed in a motor accident at Windsor, 3rd September, 1915.

RAMSAY, KENNETH MATTHEW ARNST. School period: September, 1912, to July, 1915. Captain, R.A.F. May, 1917, to March, 1919. France.

RAMSAY, NORMAN BARCLAY. School period: November, 1908, to April, 1912. Lieutenant, R.N. Armoured Cars, 1914 to 1916; R.H.A., 1917 to 1918; R.A.S.C., 1918 to 1919.

READ, CHARLES WILLIAM. School period: April, 1903, to April, 1905. Trooper, Herts. Yeomanry.

REDRUP, GEORGE JOHN. School period: March, 1887, to December, 1888. King's Royal Rifles. February, 1915, to February, 1919. France. Served in the Boer War (Queen's Medal and King Edward's Medal, with bars).

REEVES, VERNON LEONARD. School period: September, 1908, to April, 1912. Sergeant-Mechanic, R.F.C. Four years. France.

REYNOLDS, THOMAS. School period: September, 1912, to December, 1917. Flight Cadet, R.A.F. January, 1918, to February, 1919.

REYNOLDS, WILLIAM. School period: September, 1909, to April, 1912. Second Lieutenant, H.A.C. and 1st (Res.) London Regiment. December, 1915, to January, 1919.

RICHARDS, HAROLD FREDERICK. School period: September, 1914, to September, 1917. Private, Artists' Rifles O.T.C.

RICHARDSON, KASTIAN CHARLES. School period: September, 1908, to April, 1910. Guardsman, Grenadier Guards.

RICHARDSON, WILLIAM DONALD. School period: September, 1912, to July, 1916. Wireless Operator, Merchant Service. Torpedoed, 21st June, 1918, in the North Sea.

RIDGEWAY, RALPH STANLEY. School period: September, 1908, to December, 1910. Rifleman, 9th London Regiment. Enlisted September, 1914; killed in action near Wulverghem, 27th February, 1915.

ROBBINS, CHARLES ROBINSON. School period: September, 1907, to December, 1910. Captain, University and Public Schools Battalion, R.F.A. and R.F.C. Five years. France. Awarded M.C. "for general good service," 1916, and D.F.C., 1918.

ROBBINS, ERIC. School period: January, 1908, to July, 1909. Lieutenant, Northumberland Fusiliers. Five years. France.

ROBBINS, HARRY. School period: January, 1898, to December, 1902. Lieutenant, R.N.R. Five years. Dardanelles and North Sea.

ROBBINS, TOM WILTSHIRE. School period: April, 1900, to July, 1908. Surgeon Lieutenant, R.N. Three years, six months. Mediterranean.

ROBERTS, ALBERT PERCY. School period: March, 1906, to July, 1914. Second Lieutenant (Observer), R.A.F. Two years, six months.

ROBERTS, ARTHUR VICTOR INGLEBY. School period: January, 1913, to July, 1914. Lieutenant, R.A.F. Three years, six months. France.

RODEN, FRANK HAROLD. School period: September, 1908, to December, 1911. Private, 13th London Regiment and R.A.F. Four years, six months. France, Salonica, Palestine and Egypt.

ROGERS, HERBERT HANWELL. School period: September, 1911, to September, 1914. Lance-Corporal, Queen's Westminster Rifles. Two years, six months. France.

ROGERS, REGINALD GORDON. School period: May, 1908, to July, 1911. Captain, 4th Gordon Highlanders, attached King's African Rifles. December, 1914, to May, 1919. France and East Africa. Wounded, September, 1915.

ROGERS, SIDNEY. School period: March, 1907, to April, 1910. Corporal, London Electrical Engineers, R.E. Four years, ten months.

ROLFE, WILLIAM ALFRED THOMAS. School period: April, 1909, to July, 1910. Trooper, Herts. Yeomanry and Machine Gun Corps (Cavalry). May, 1915, to January, 1919. Egypt and Palestine.

ROUTLEDGE, LESLIE HERBERT. School period: September, 1901, to December, 1909. Rifleman, 12th London Regiment. Enlisted at outbreak of war and went to France in December, 1914; wounded, 8th May, 1915, and reported missing, presumed killed.

ROWORTH, ALAN. School period: September, 1907, to December, 1910. Second Lieutenant, Machine Gun Corps. August, 1914, to March, 1919. France. Awarded M.M., October, 1917 (Passchendaele); mentioned in despatches, 1919.

RUSSELL, FRANK. School period: September, 1905, to July, 1910. Private, 7th Middlesex Regiment. Killed in action, 16th September, 1916, after two years' service.

RYDING, JOHN THACKERAY. School period: May, 1899, to July, 1903. Second Lieutenant.

SALTWELL, EDWARD JOSEPH. School period: September, 1902, to December, 1906. Staff-Captain, R.F.A. Enlisted September, 1914; promoted Captain and Adjutant, April, 1917; awarded M.C., October, 1918; also mentioned in despatches.

SANSOM, EDWARD JOHN. School period: September, 1900, to December, 1904. Sergeant-Major, 17th Canadians, attached Canadian Army Gym. Staff. January, 1915, to March, 1919.

SARGENT, WILLIAM PERCIVAL. School period: February, 1896, to December, 1900. Rifleman, Queen's Westminster Rifles. Two years. Wounded on the Somme, 1916; discharged November, 1917.

SAUNDERSON, GEORGE HERBERT. School period: September, 1909, to July, 1912. Sergeant-Instructor (Bombing and Lewis Gun). 1st Herts. Regiment, attached 10th Corps School. August, 1914, to January, 1919. France.

SAWYER, ARTHUR EDMUND. School period: January, 1906, to March, 1914. Private, Civil Service Rifles. February, 1915, to November, 1918. France, Salonica and Palestine. Wounded, January, 1918.

SAYER, HAROLD HARRY. School period: September, 1905, to July, 1909. Private, 17th and 11th Essex Regiment. Discharged on account of wounds, July, 1919.

SCHORN, EDWIN JOHN. School period: January, 1911, to July, 1912. Rifleman, 5th Royal Scots Regiment.

SCOTT, EDWARD ANDERSON. School period: May to December, 1910. Norfolk Regiment.

SEABROOK, EDWARD DARBY. School period: September, 1902, to July, 1905. Lieutenant, R.F.A. August, 1914, to August, 1919. Served as Sergeant in Herts. R.F.A. until August, 1916; commissioned while in Egypt and sent to Salonica; posted to 115th Brigade, R.F.A.

SEAR, CYRIL JAMES. School period: May, 1910, to April, 1917. Second Lieutenant, R.A.F. May, 1917, to April, 1919.

SEAR, FREDERICK WILLIAM GEORGE. School period: February, 1900, to April, 1905. 2nd Class Petty Officer, R.N. Sick Berth Staff. November, 1915, to November, 1919. Mediterranean.

SEAR, SIDNEY HERBERT. School period: January, 1902, to April, 1907. Private, R.A.M.C. Killed at Pilkem Ridge, October, 1917.

SEAR, WILLIAM ALFRED. School period: January, 1907, to December, 1909. Petty Officer, R.N.A.S., transferred April, 1918, to R.A.F., Sergeant. Three years, ten months.

SEYMOUR, FRANK HAROLD. School period: May, 1911, to July, 1912. Private, 15th London Regiment.

SEYMOUR, NOEL DENNIS. School period: September, 1911, to December, 1914. 1st Herts. Regiment.

SHARMAN, CYRIL THOMAS. School period: September, 1903, to July, 1910. Captain, 6th Notts. and Derby Regiment (Sherwood Foresters). September, 1914, to February, 1920.

SHAW, JOHN ERIC. School period: September, 1906, to July, 1911. Petty Officer, R.N.A.S. July, 1915, to February, 1919.

SIMMONDS, FREDERICK. School period: May, 1914, to April, 1916. Private, 11th Royal Fusiliers. Wounded on the Somme; awarded Croix de Guerre for saving the life of a French officer under fire.

SIMMONDS, HENRY ARTHUR THOMAS. School period: September, 1908, to July, 1913. Lieutenant, Machine Gun Corps. Five years. France.

SIMMONS, STANLEY EDWARD. School period: January, 1913, to July, 1916. Private, Machine Cun Corps. September, 1916, to February, 1919. France. Gassed in August, 1918, on the La Bassée front.

SIMMONS, THOMAS HERBERT. School period: September, 1906, to July, 1907. Captain, Civil Service Rifles. Three years, six months. France. Wounded on the Somme.

SIMMS, ALFRED EDWARD. School period: April to December, 1912. 2nd Class Air Mechanic, R.F.C.

SIMPSON, OSWALD GIVAN EWART. School period: April, 1901, to July, 1905. Captain, RA.M.C. Five years.

SKILTON, EDWARD ALAN. School period: April, 1902, to December, 1910. Rifleman, London Rifle Brigade. Two years. France. Discharged, as medically unfit, June, 1916.

SKINNER, JOHN WILLIAM. Member of the Staff: September, 1913, to July, 1914. Lieutenant, Duke of Cornwall's Light Infantry. Three years. Mentioned in despatches during service with Egyptian Expeditionary Force.

SLADE, EDWARD FRED. School period: September, 1905, to December, 1907. Rifleman, 9th London Regiment. Drowned in France, August, 1915.

SLANEY, WILLIAM EDWIN. School period: September, 1910, to May, 1913. Signaller, R.F.A. (386th Battery). Four years. Mesopotamia.

SMITH, ARTHUR LYON. School period: April, 1900, to July, 1908. Corporal, 2nd Special Brigade, R.E., transferred from 4th Bedfordshire Regiment. Four years. France.

SMITH, EDWIN MAURICE. School period: April, 1909, to June, 1918. Private, Artists' Rifles O.T.C. Six months.

SMITH, GEORGE BOREHAM. School period: March to December, 1908. Rifleman, 9th London Regiment. Killed in action, 24th June, 1917.

SMITH, GEORGE EDWARD. School period: September, 1909, to July, 1913. Rifleman, London Rifle Brigade. September, 1914, to January, 1919.

SMITH, GILBERT GEORGE. School period: January, 1905, to July, 1908. Company Quarter-Master Sergeant, R.E. Three years, three months.

SMITH, HERBERT HAGLEWOOD. School period: September, 1910, to July, 1913. Signalman, Royal Naval Division. Four years. At Battle of Jutland and mine-sweeping in the Mediterranean.

SMITH, JOHN CYRIL. School period: September, 1907, to April, 1910. Squadron Sergeant-Major, Herts. Yeomanry.

SMITH, RALPH. School period September, 1909, to December, 1911. Private, 4th Bedfordshire Regiment. December, 1915, to March, 1917. France. Wounded August, 1916, and in hospital until discharged as unfit.

SMITH, REGINALD FREDERICK. School period: September, 1909, to November, 1915. Second Lieutenant, Civil Service Rifles. Killed in action, 22nd May, 1917.

SNARE, DANIEL THOMAS JOSIAH. School period: April, 1884, to August, 1888. Private, Royal West Kent Regiment. Killed in action, 18th April, 1916.

SOUTHERN, FREDERIC JOHN. School period: October, 1897, to December, 1901. Lance-Corporal, H.A.C. until commissioned in 4th Essex Regiment, December, 1916. Sniping and Intelligence Officer to 13th Essex Regiment in France, 1917; severely wounded at Cambrai, December, 1917. Four years.

SPARKS, JOHN HENRY. School period: January, 1906, to December, 1912. Private, London Rifle Brigade and 13th London Regiment (Kensingtons). 1916 to 1919. France, Salonica and Palestine. Wounded, 1916.

SPENCER, EDWARD LEONARD. School period: September, 1908, to July, 1910. Lieutenant, 21st London Regiment (1st Surrey Rifles). Four years, nine months. France.

SPICER, ARTHUR CHARLES. School period: March, 1889, to December, 1892. Lieutenant, Essex Regiment.

SPICER, PERCY HENRY. School period: January, 1900, to July, 1906. Private, 1st Surrey Regiment.

SPILMAN, CHARLES ROBERT. School period: January, 1908, to July, 1914. Ordinary Seaman, R.N. One year, six months.

SQUIRE, GEOFFREY WILLIAM. School period: September, 1910, to October, 1914. Driver, 2/3rd London R.F.A. April, 1915, to March, 1919. France. Employed as Draughtsman (Barrage Maps) at H.Q., 58th D.A.

SQUIRE, LEONARD PERCY. School period: September, 1911, to March, 1916. Flight-Cadet, R.A.F. Killed as result of accident due to engine trouble while flying near Lincoln.

STADDON, FREDERIC FRANK WHITE. School period: September, 1910, to May, 1913. Lance-Corporal, Civil Service Rifles. Four years. France.

STEVENS, CYRIL WALTER. School period: September, 1905, to July, 1909. Captain, 93rd Burmah Infantry. Enlisted in Artists' Rifles, August, 1914; France. March, 1915, Second Lieutenant, 2nd Scottish Rifles. March, 1918, Burmah Infantry; India.

STEVENS, HAROLD JAMES. School period: April, 1902, to July, 1904. Lieutenant and Quarter-Master, R.G.A. Five years, four months.

STEVENS, WILLIAM FREDERICK THOMAS. School period: September, 1910, to December, 1913. Private, East Surrey Regiment. May, 1916, to January, 1919. Awarded M.M. (London Gazette, 17th June, 1919).

ST. LEGER, ROBERT CECIL. School period: November, 1902, to July, 1905. Private, West Surrey Regiment. Four years.

STIRLING, JAMES. School period: November, 1902, to July, 1905. Private, London Scottish. Two years. France. Discharged as medically unfit.

STOTT, EDWARD BLEACKLEY. School period: June, 1912, to June, 1915. Private, 5th Royal Warwickshire Regiment. Died of pneumonia, 12th October, 1918.

STRUGNELL, ALFRED CHARLES. School period: January, 1903, to July, 1906. Lieutenant, 2nd Yorkshire Regiment; had previously served for ten years in 16th Lancers. Killed in action in France, 1st July, 1916.

STURMAN, FREDERICK CHARLES. School period: September, 1907, to July, 1911. Lieutenant, 17th Manchester Regiment. Three years, ten months. Discharged, through ill-health contracted on active service, 23rd May, 1918.

SUMNER, GEORGE HUBBARD. School period: April, 1909. to July, 1914. Trooper, 21st Lancers. Three years, seven months. India.

SUTHERLAND, RUPERT REGINALD JOHN. School period: September, 1907, to July, 1918. Private, H.A.C. September, 1918, to January, 1919.

SWABEY, JESSE LESLIE WATKINS. School period: January, 1905, to December, 1907. Second Lieutenant, 1st London Regiment.

SYGROVE, ALBERT. School period: September, 1909, to July, 1912. Gunner, R.H.A. 1914 to 1919. Western Front.

SYGROVE, ARTHUR JAMES. School period: September, 1908, to July, 1911. Private, R.A.S.C. (M.T.). Three years. Mesopotamia.

SYGROVE, JOHN WILLIAM. School period: January, 1903, to July, 1906. Corporal, R.F.A. Four years, six months. France.

TAIT, JAMES WILLIAM. School period: May, 1908, to July, 1915. Cadet, Artists' Rifles O.T.C.

TAPPLY, REGINALD LANGFORD. School period: January, 1897, to May, 1904. Corporal, R.E. Two years.

TAPPLY, ROBERT HUNTER. School period: March, 1906, to July, 1912. Sergeant, R.E. Three years. France.

TAPSTER, ALFRED CHARLES. School period: September, 1906, to April, 1910. Lieutenant, R.N.A.S. and R.A.F. Four years.

TAPSTER, ALBERT GEORGE. School period: September, 1904, to July, 1909. Lieutenant, R.E., East Anglian Company. Four years, six months. Mesopotamia.

TATTON, ERIC HUDSON. School period: September, 1904, to December, 1910. Captain and Flight Commander, R.A.F. Enlisted August, 1914; commission in East Yorkshire Regiment, January, 1915. Egypt and France. Transferred to R.A.F., 1917; killed in action, 20th April, 1918.

TAYLOR, ARTHUR FREDERICK. School period: February, 1904, to December, 1908. Sergeant, H.A.C. Four years. France.

TAYLOR, CHARLES ERNEST. School period: March, 1890, to April, 1895. 2nd Air Mechanic, R.N.A.S. 1917 to 1919.

TAYLOR, REGINALD CHARLES. School period: September, 1914, to December, 1915. Able Seaman, R.N. February, 1916, to December, 1918. West Coast of Africa and North Sea.

TEARLE, WILLIAM EDWARD. School period: September, 1912, to July, 1915. Sergeant-Observer, R.N.A.S., and R.A.F. One year, six months.

THOMAS, WILLIAM RUSSELL. School period: May, 1899, to December, 1905. Corporal (Bomber), R.A.F., transferred from R.N.A.S. 1915 to 1919. France.

THORN, GEORGE. School period: January, 1902, to July, 1909. Lieutenant, Indian Army. Four years, seven months. Cameroons (West Africa). Mesopotamia, India and South Africa.

TIPPEN, LEWIS ROLAND. School period: April, 1898, to December, 1899. Assistant Paymaster, R.N. Entered Navy in July, 1908; drowned in H.M.S. "Invincible," in Battle of Jutland, 31st May, 1916.

TOMPKINS, CYRIL ARTHUR. School period: September, 1910, to July, 1913. Lewis Gunner, Bedfordshire Regiment. Enlisted in April, 1917, in 3rd Suffolks; transferred to 1st Bedfordshires. Italy and France. Killed in action at Achiet-le-Petit, 23rd August, 1918.

TOOVEY, JAMES ROWLAND. School period: January, 1907, to July, 1913. Sapper, 5th Field Survey Company, R.E. Two years. France.

TRACY, CECIL JOHN. School period: September, 1891, to December, 1897. Driver, R.A.S.C. (M.T.). Drowned in France,

May, 1916; had served in German South-West Africa as Quarter-Master Sergeant.

TRIPP, VICTOR HENRY. School period: September, 1906, to July, 1908. Lieutenant, A.S.C.

TUCKER, WILLIAM EDWARD. School period: March, 1894, to December, 1896. Private, 10th Canadians. Killed in action on the Somme, 26th September, 1916.

TULEY, VICTOR CHARLES. School period: January, 1896, to April, 1898. Lieutenant, R.E. May, 1915, to July, 1919. France.

TURNER, EDRIC VICTOR. School period: September, 1902, to July, 1912. R.A.M.C.

TWIGGER, ARTHUR EDGAR. School period: January, 1897, to June, 1899. Sergeant, R.E., Inland Water Transport Section. Three years, two months. Overseas, July, 1916, to December, 1918.

UNITT, FRANCIS VICTOR. School period: September, 1912, to December, 1915. Wireless Operator.

VALE, CYRIL SIDNEY MERRALLS. School period: January, 1907, to December, 1914. Private, Herts. Regiment. Died of wounds, 27th August, 1918.

VASEY, HAROLD LESLIE. School period: September, 1908, to April, 1912. Sergeant, Royal Fusiliers. November, 1915, to June, 1919.

VINE, WALTER JAMES. School period: April, 1906, to July, 1907. Corporal, 3rd Royal Fusiliers and R.E. France. 1914 to 1919.

VOSS, CHARLES JOSEPH. School period: January, 1889, to March, 1892. Corporal, Royal Sussex Regiment. December, 1915, to April, 1919.

WALKER, WILLIAM ALBERT. School period: September, 1908, to December, 1912. Private, 2nd H.A.C. (Infantry). December, 1915, to July, 1918. France. Wounded, February, 1917; discharged as unfit.

WARD, CHARLES EDWARD. School period: September, 1908, to December, 1912. Captain, R.A.F. Four years.

WARREN, ERNEST ALFRED. School period: September, 1907, to July, 1911. Private, 15th London Regiment; transferred to 19th London Regiment. January, 1916, to April, 1918. Wounded in Somme battle, 29th September, 1916.

WARREN, FRANK FULCHER. School period: September, 1906, to July, 1909. Private, Civil Service Rifles. Enlisted January, 1916; killed in action at High Wood, 15th September, 1916.

WARREN, HERBERT CHARLES. School period: September, 1904, to July, 1907. Corporal, A.O.C., transferred to 1st Dorsetshire Regiment. November, 1915, to July, 1919. France and Belgium. Wounded at Ors, 4th November, 1918.

WATERHOUSE, ARNOLD MIDDLETON. School period: September, 1900, to July, 1907. Private, 1st Surrey Regiment; 21st City of London Regiment. Enlisted in August, 1914; killed in action at Givenchy, 26th May, 1915.

WATERHOUSE, DAVID STANLEY. School period: January, 1898, to July, 1906. Lieutenant, British South African Police, Service Column, Northern Rhodesian Regiment. Served all through the campaigns in German South-West Africa and German East Africa. Mentioned in despatches, 30th September, 1918, "for gallant and distinguished service in the Field." [Has since died at Gwelo, Rhodesia, on 6th February, 1921, of Blackwater Fever, contracted on war service.]

WATERHOUSE, HAROLD. School period: September, 1903, to June, 1911. Lieutenant, R.G.A. December, 1914, to end of War. Served with the H.A.C. in France before receiving commission. Wounded in the Ypres salient.

WATSON, CLEMENT SPENCER. School period: September, 1907, to July, 1912. Sergeant, Royal Fusiliers (London Regiment). Enlisted September, 1914. Malta, Gallipoli, and France. Died of wounds, 18th May, 1917.

WATSON, WILLIAM NEVILLE. School period: September, 1911, to March, 1915. Rifleman, Civil Service Rifles. Joined London Rifle Brigade in August, 1917; went to France and was there drafted to Civil Service Rifles; died of wounds, 26th August, 1918.

WATT, PERCY NEWTON. School period: April, 1907, to May, 1913. C.Q.M.S., 2nd King's Own Royal Lancaster Regiment. Three years, six months. Dardanelles and Salonica. Mentioned in despatches.

WATT, RICHARD BRIND. School period: September, 1908, to July, 1915. Corporal, 1st King's Royal Rifle Corps. 1918 to 1920.

WEBB, STAFFORD. School period: September, 1908, to April, 1912. Captain, Middlesex Regiment. March, 1914, to September, 1919. Served with the Civil Service Rifles until May, 1915; three times wounded.

WELLAND, RALPH JOHN HIBBERT. School period: September, 1907, to November, 1911. Lieutenant, Herts. Yeomanry, 13th London Regiment, Seaforth Highlanders, R.A.V.C., R.F.A., R.G.A. Five years, six months.

WELLER, GEORGE HERBERT. School period: September, 1895, to July, 1897. Staff Captain, H.L.I. Killed in action in Gallipoli, 12th July, 1915.

WELLER, JOHN ADRIAN. School period: September, 1895, to January, 1896. Second Lieutenant, R.F.C. and R.A.F. France. Wounded in aerial combat, 25th August, 1918.

WELLINGS, NORMAN. School period: September, 1903, to July, 1908. Sergeant, 5th West Kent Regiment.

WHEELER, CHARLES HADLEY. School period: September, 1911, to December, 1913. Second Lieutenant, R.A.F. Two years. France.

WHEELER, DENIS. School period: January, 1891, to July, 1896. Private, 2/8th Worcestershire Regiment. Two years. France. Wounded August, 1917.

WHEWAY, GEORGE HENRY. School period: September, 1905, to July, 1907. Private, R.A.S.C.

WHITAKER, GEORGE. School period: September, 1900, to April, 1902. R.H.A.

WHITCHER, HAROLD GEORGE. School period: October, 1897, to July, 1901. Despatch Rider.

WHITE, HENRY ALBERT. School period: September, 1908, to March, 1911. Lance-Corporal, Army Pay Corps.

WHITEHORN, JAMES WILFRED. School period: September, 1907, to July, 1910. Private, 1st Bedfordshire Regiment. Enlisted September, 1914. France. Killed on Hill 60, 20th April, 1915

WIGGS, JOHN REGINALD. School period: September, 1896, to July, 1903. Lieutenant, 14th Cheshire Regiment. Joined R.N., 1915; transferred to Army, 1916. France. Invalided out, 1917.

WIGGS, JOSEPH CHARLES. School period: September, 1903, to April, 1907. Lieutenant, 9th Royal Sussex Regiment. September, 1914, to January, 1920. Gallipoli, Egypt, and France. Twice wounded.

WIGGS, REGINALD HENRY. School period: September, 1908, to July, 1911. Corporal, 1st Coldstream Guards. November, 1914, to March, 1919. France and Belgium.

WIGGS, WALTER. School period: January, 1904, to July, 1907. Private, Civil Service Rifles. Four years. Brigade Sharpshooter and Observer for three years.

WILD, CHARLES JAMES. School period: September, 1894, to July, 1900. Paymaster Sub-Lieutenant, R.N.R. Four years, six months. Battle of Jutland.

WILD, EDWARD WHITTINGTON. School period: February, 1902, to December, 1906. Able Seaman, R.N.V.R. August, 1914, to March, 1919. Battle of Jutland.

WILD, FRANK WHITTINGTON. School period: January, 1899, to July, 1900. C.Q.M.S, R.E. Three years, seven months. France.

WILD, HERBERT WILLIAM. School period: September, 1900, to July, 1904. R.N. January, 1917, to end of War. Portsmouth Escort Flotilla.

WILD, JOHN SYDNEY. School period: January, 1897, to July, 1898. Sapper, R.E. (Railway Transport Section). Three years, eight months. Salonica.

WILD, SAMUEL THOMAS. School period: September, 1891, to July, 1892. Sapper, R.E. (Transportation). Four years. France.

WILD, WALTER. School period: January, 1894, to October, 1898. Sergeant, Queen's Westminster Rifles. August, 1914, to March, 1919. France, 1914; wounded on the Somme, 1916, and again September, 1917.

WILLIAMS, ALFRED RICHARD. School period: September, 1904, to July, 1907. Private, 17th Royal Fusiliers. Enlisted in 1914; in 1917 received commission and appointed to 49th Machine Gun Corps, attached 16th (Irish) Division; killed in action on Frezenberg Ridge, 16th August, 1917.

WILLIAMS, BRIAN. School period: October, 1894, to July, 1897, and January, 1902, to July, 1903. Lance-Corporal, Army Service Corps (Motor Transport). France. 1915 to 1919.

WILLIAMS, HERBERT HAROLD. School period: April, 1909, to December, 1912. Rifleman, King's Royal Rifle Corps from May, 1918. France.

WILLIMAN, ALBERT EDWARD. School period: September, 1901, to July, 1906. Sapper; London Electrical Engineers, Tank Corps. November, 1915, to end of War.

WILLIS, ALEXANDER GALBRAITH FLEMING. Member of the Staff since September, 1912. Lieutenant, 2nd The Buffs. January, 1915, to July, 1916, 16th Middlesex Regiment, France; August, 1916, to February, 1919, 2nd The Buffs, Salonica.

WILSON, ALFRED JOHN. School period: January, 1908, to April, 1910. Leading Mechanic, R.N.A.S. Three years, ten months.

WILSON, ARTHUR. School period: January, 1899, to June, 1909. Private, 7th East Kent Regiment. One year, ten months. Killed at Montauban, near Albert, 1st July, 1916.

WILSON, CHARLES TAPPLY. School period: January, 1904, July, 1912. Private, 214th and 28th Canadians. 1916 to 1919. France.

WILSON, HUMPHREY. School period: January, 1909, to April, 1912. Lieutenant, Machine Gun Corps.

WILSON, JAMES. School period: January, 1898, to April, 1905. Sergeant, Herts. Yeomanry. 1914 to 1919. Mesopotamia.

WILSON, JOSEPH ALEC. School period: September, 1908, to July, 1910. Lieutenant, Machine Gun Corps. One year, seven months. Joined McGill University Company and sent to Princess Patricia's Regiment with reinforcements; gained commission from the trenches into 15th Northumberland Fusiliers, afterwards transferred to M.G.C.; killed in action, 14th November, 1916.

WILSON, WILLIAM. School period: September, 1898, to April, 1905. Private, H.A.C. Two years.

WISE, ARTHUR CHARLES. School period: September, 1907, to July, 1911. Private, 1st London Regiment (Royal Fusiliers).

WOOD, ALFRED BRUCE. School period: September, 1911, to December, 1913. Private, London Scottish and Queen's Royal West Surrey Regiment. Three years. France.

WOOD, DONALD JAMES. School period: January, 1909, to February, 1913. Lance-Corporal, London Scottish. Three years, six months. France, Salonica and Palestine.

WOOD, JOSEPH CHARLES. School period: September, 1910, to July, 1913. Second Lieutenant, 3rd London Regiment (Royal Fusiliers). Enlisted in London Rifle Brigade. Two years. France.

WOOD, ROBERT. Member of the Staff since September, 1904. Major, R.G.A. Commission, August, 1916; France, 1917 to 1918; commanding 5th Siege Battery, May to October, 1918.

WOODMAN, GILBERT DANIEL. School period: March, 1908, to December, 1910. Trumpeter, D/23rd (Army) Brigade R.F.A. (T.). Five years.

WOODS, WALTER HENRY STEVENS. School period: January, 1899, to April, 1900. Second Lieutenant, 5th Middlesex Regiment. August, 1914, to January, 1919. Wounded at La Clytte (Kemmel), 8th July, 1918.

WOODWARD, FREDERICK. School period: September, 1904, to July, 1907. Private, Herts. Regiment. 1914 to 1917. France. Wounded at Battle of Ancre, 13th November, 1916; discharged owing to wounds.

WOOLMAN, EBENEZER. School period: September, 1896, to July, 1901. Captain, 128th Overseas Battalion. 1916 to 1918.

WOOLMAN, JOHN GRAY. School period: September, 1904, to May, 1909. Second Lieutenant, 3rd York and Lancs. Regiment. Joined Inns of Court O.T.C. in December, 1916; gazetted to 3rd York and Lancs. in September, 1917; April, 1918, went to France with 1/4th York and Lancs.; killed in action near Valenciennes, 2nd November, 1918.

WOOLMAN, MARK. School period: April, 1902, to July, 1911. Corporal, Australian Imperial Force. 1915 to 1919. Contracted malaria and pneumonia in Egypt; was wounded and gassed in France; later attached to Headquarters, 1st Division Australian Imperial Forces, as Observer.

WORSFOLD, VICTOR GEORGE. School period: September, 1898, to April, 1904. Private, Civil Service Rifles; then Sergeant-Instructor and Lecturer, 19th Corps. Three years, six months.

WRIGHT, FRANK. School period: September, 1910, to July, 1913. Trooper, 13th Hussars. October, 1915, to December, 1919. Mesopotamia and India.

WRIGHT, WILLIAM. School period: September, 1888, to December, 1896. Second Lieutenant: London Rifle Brigade, King's Royal Rifles, R.F.C. Three years.

WYKES, CHARLES EDGAR. School period: February, 1900, to April, 1901. Lieutenant, R.A.F. Killed in action in France, 13th August, 1918.

WYKES, RONALD ARTHUR. School period: January, 1905, to July, 1909. Captain, 2nd Devons. Joined Artists' Rifles in August, 1914; three years in France; wounded at the Hohenzollern Redoubt.

YOUNG, ALBERT FRANKLIN. School period: September, 1913, to March, 1915. 1st Air Mechanic, R.F.C. (Wireless Section). Wounded in France, March, 1918, when his aerodrome was bombed. Died in hospital in London, 9th June, 1918.

ZAMMETT, WILLIAM ARTHUR JOHN. School period: September, 1910, to July, 1913. Grenadier Guards.

DECORATIONS

DISTINGUISHED SERVICE ORDER

Ashwanden, S. W. L.
Palmer, A.

MILITARY CROSS AND BAR

Heather, T. W.

MILITARY CROSS

Barton-Smith, F.
Batcheldor, W.
Cass, W. D.
Collins, H. J.
Davies, T. H.
Harvey, W. S.
James, L. E.
Morton, F. W.
Newcombe, F. G.
Norman, S. O.
Paterson, F. J.
Robbins, C. R.
Saltwell, E. J.

DISTINGUISHED FLYING CROSS

Moorhouse, J. D.
Oxley, A. R.
Robbins, C. R.

AIR FORCE CROSS

Chamberlin, T. C.

DISTINGUISHED CONDUCT MEDAL

De'Ath, E.
French, C. J.
Hawkins, W. J.
Longthorne, W. G.

MILITARY MEDAL

Fayers, S.
Hawker, W. J. E.
Judge, S. R.
Lloyd, H. G.
Longthorne, W. G.
Morse, H. E.
Phillips, F. G.
Roworth, A.
Stevens, W. F. T.

MERITORIOUS SERVICE MEDAL

Kirkman, A. H. W.

CROIX DE GUERRE (France)

Simmonds, F.

MEDAILLE MILITAIRE

Farley, E.

SERBIAN SILVER MEDAL

Callard, H. J. P.

SILVER MEDAL FOR GALLANTRY

Awarded by Provisional North Russian Government (to be worn with ribbon of Order of St. Stanislav).

Martin, A. L. A.

MENTIONED IN DESPATCHES

(not included above.)

Burrell, C. R.
Franklin, R. H.
Franklin, S. S.
Gardiner, A. T.
Pallett, E.
Skinner, J. W.
Waterhouse, D. S.
Watt, P. N.

www.ingramcontent.com/pod-product-compliance
Ingram Content Group UK Ltd.
Pitfield, Milton Keynes, MK11 3LW, UK
UKHW041845190726
13854UKWH00002B/717

9 781843 424246